Prohibition: A Very Short Introduction

VERY SHORT INTRODUCTIONS are for anyone wanting a stimulating and accessible way into a new subject. They are written by experts, and have been translated into more than 45 different languages.

The series began in 1995, and now covers a wide variety of topics in every discipline. The VSI library currently contains over 550 volumes—a Very Short Introduction to everything from Psychology and Philosophy of Science to American History and Relativity—and continues to grow in every subject area.

Very Short Introductions available now:

ABOLITIONISM Richard S. Newman
THE ABRAHAMIC RELIGIONS
    Charles L. Cohen
ACCOUNTING Christopher Nobes
ADAM SMITH Christopher J. Berry
ADOLESCENCE Peter K. Smith
ADVERTISING Winston Fletcher
AESTHETICS Bence Nanay
AFRICAN AMERICAN RELIGION
    Eddie S. Glaude Jr
AFRICAN HISTORY John Parker and
    Richard Rathbone
AFRICAN POLITICS Ian Taylor
AFRICAN RELIGIONS
    Jacob K. Olupona
AGEING Nancy A. Pachana
AGNOSTICISM Robin Le Poidevin
AGRICULTURE Paul Brassley and
    Richard Soffe
ALEXANDER THE GREAT
    Hugh Bowden
ALGEBRA Peter M. Higgins
AMERICAN CULTURAL
    HISTORY Eric Avila
AMERICAN FOREIGN RELATIONS
    Andrew Preston
AMERICAN HISTORY Paul S. Boyer
AMERICAN IMMIGRATION
    David A. Gerber
AMERICAN LEGAL HISTORY
    G. Edward White
AMERICAN NAVAL HISTORY
    Craig L. Symonds
AMERICAN POLITICAL HISTORY
    Donald Critchlow

AMERICAN POLITICAL PARTIES
    AND ELECTIONS L. Sandy Maisel
AMERICAN POLITICS
    Richard M. Valelly
THE AMERICAN PRESIDENCY
    Charles O. Jones
THE AMERICAN REVOLUTION
    Robert J. Allison
AMERICAN SLAVERY
    Heather Andrea Williams
THE AMERICAN WEST Stephen Aron
AMERICAN WOMEN'S HISTORY
    Susan Ware
ANAESTHESIA Aidan O'Donnell
ANALYTIC PHILOSOPHY
    Michael Beaney
ANARCHISM Colin Ward
ANCIENT ASSYRIA Karen Radner
ANCIENT EGYPT Ian Shaw
ANCIENT EGYPTIAN ART AND
    ARCHITECTURE Christina Riggs
ANCIENT GREECE Paul Cartledge
THE ANCIENT NEAR EAST
    Amanda H. Podany
ANCIENT PHILOSOPHY Julia Annas
ANCIENT WARFARE Harry Sidebottom
ANGELS David Albert Jones
ANGLICANISM Mark Chapman
THE ANGLO-SAXON AGE John Blair
ANIMAL BEHAVIOUR
    Tristram D. Wyatt
THE ANIMAL KINGDOM
    Peter Holland
ANIMAL RIGHTS David DeGrazia
THE ANTARCTIC Klaus Dodds

Available soon:

For more information visit our web site

www.oup.com/vsi/

W. J. Rorabaugh

PROHIBITION

A Very Short Introduction

OXFORD
UNIVERSITY PRESS

OXFORD
UNIVERSITY PRESS

Oxford University Press is a department of the University of Oxford.
It furthers the University's objective of excellence in research, scholarship,
and education by publishing worldwide. Oxford is a registered trade mark of
Oxford University Press in the UK and certain other countries.

Published in the United States of America by Oxford University Press
198 Madison Avenue, New York, NY 10016, United States of America.

© Oxford University Press 2018, 2020

Published in hardcover as *Prohibition: A Concise History* in 2018

Library of Congress Control Number: 2019948404

ISBN 978–0–19–028010–9

1 3 5 7 9 8 6 4 2

Printed in Great Britain
by Ashford Colour Press Ltd., Gosport, Hants.

Contents

Acknowledgments

My curiosity about prohibition began early in life, when I had to negotiate the cultural differences between my mother's wet family and my father's dry family. During prohibition my maternal grandfather made wine in the basement from Concord grapes grown in the backyard. My mother later described the product as awful. When I was a child, my mother occasionally took a drink, but my father never did. My abstinent paternal grandfather had always declared that he would try alcohol at age seventy-five. On his seventy-fifth birthday, the neighbors in the small town where he lived gathered on his front porch, knocked on the door, and presented him with a half pint of whiskey. He took one sip, set the bottle on the porch rail, muttered that he had not missed a thing, went back inside, and closed the door. His was a short drinking career.

My interest in alcohol led to my book *The Alcoholic Republic* (1979), to other research in alcohol history, and now to this short history of prohibition. I am grateful to the many scholars whose works have helped make this synthesis possible. They are cited in the References and Further Reading. Anand Yang, the chair of the History Department at the University of Washington, provided a teaching schedule that eased the writing of this book. I would like to thank Donald Critchlow and the anonymous readers for Oxford University Press for their insights on earlier drafts. I am indebted to both Nancy Toff and Elizabeth Vaziri at Oxford University Press. In particular, Nancy has been a model editor at every stage of the process. For help with photographs, I would like to thank the staffs at the Denver Public Library, Indiana Historical Society, Kansas State Historical Society, Ohio Historical Society, and Wisconsin Historical Society.

List of illustrations

Introduction

From 1920 to 1933, the Eighteenth Amendment to the United States Constitution banned the production, sale, or transportation of alcoholic beverages. This book is about both prohibition and the century-long campaign that led to that result. The American dry movement was part of a global effort to ban or control alcohol and other drugs. This worldwide effort against pleasurable but addictive and often destructive substances began with the Enlightenment, gained strength during religious-based moral uplift and industrialization in the 1800s, and peaked after 1900 amid rising concerns about public health, family problems, and the power of producers to entice overuse. Many of these same issues belong to the war on drugs. Global trade and imperial politics have played major roles both in the spread of alcohol and other drugs and in the battle to control or stop use.

How, then, should a government handle alcohol? Can more be gained by controls or by prohibition? Sweden adopted a state control system, and Britain long used restrictive policies to reduce consumption. Although a number of nations considered a ban, only a handful have instituted one. Prohibition seldom worked the way it was intended. For example, Russian prohibition during World War I helped bring down the tsar's regime. American prohibition also failed. The price of alcohol rose, quality fell, and consumption dropped sharply. Even during prohibition, however, many Americans continued to drink, which generated corruption and organized crime. Moonshine was dangerous, bootleggers got rich, and the government lost alcohol taxes. In 1933, a disgusted country abandoned national prohibition.

This book about American prohibition addresses several related questions: How and why did one of the hardest drinking countries decide to adopt prohibition? How did a religious-based temperance movement to stop the abuse of whiskey turn into a political crusade to stop all alcohol consumption? What role did women play in this movement? How did immigration affect drinking and the campaign against alcohol? What happened during prohibition that caused Americans to change their minds? What kind of alcohol policies were adopted when prohibition ended in 1933?

The road to prohibition began with heavy drinking in colonial times. After the American Revolution, a plentiful supply of cheap untaxed whiskey made from surplus corn on the western frontier caused alcohol consumption to soar. Whiskey cost less than beer, wine, coffee, tea, or milk, and it was safer than water. By the 1820s, the average adult white male drank a half pint of whiskey a day. Liquor corrupted elections, wife beating and child abuse were common, and many crimes were committed while the perpetrator was under the influence. Serious people wondered if the republic could survive.

The growing level of alcohol abuse provoked a backlash. Reformers, rooted in the evangelical Protestant revivals of the 1820s, urged Americans to switch from whiskey to beer or light wine. Commercial beer, however, was available only in cities, and imported wine cost too much for the average drinker. Reformers then demanded that everyone voluntarily abstain from all alcoholic beverages. By 1840, perhaps half of Americans had taken the pledge, and reformers decided that the rest of the population needed to be sober, too. Beginning with Maine in 1851, eleven states passed prohibition laws during the 1850s. These laws failed in large part because Irish and German immigrants refused to give up whiskey and beer. Alcohol policy was temporarily put aside during the Civil War.

The Woman's Christian Temperance Union (WCTU), founded in 1874, resumed the long campaign to dry out America by fighting to ban alcohol at the local, state, and national levels. Under Frances Willard, the organization also advocated women's suffrage. Until Willard's death in 1898, the WCTU was the main organization pushing anti-liquor legislation. Local option prohibition enjoyed considerable success in rural areas, where evangelical churches were strong.

In 1893, the Anti-Saloon League (ASL) joined the fight. Led by the brilliant Washington lobbyist Wayne Wheeler, the ASL mobilized voters for prohibition. The ASL elected legislators and members of Congress loyal to its agenda. The group pushed local option where it could not win statewide prohibition. Once liquor dealers were eliminated from large areas of a state, a statewide ban was easier to enact. Wheeler believed that great wet cities such as New York, Chicago, and San Francisco eventually could be dried out by encirclement. Prohibition then could be made permanent with a national constitutional amendment.

To defeat ASL-backed dry candidates, wet opponents took money from brewers, who made hidden donations through the German-American Alliance, an immigrant organization with two million members. When World War I began in 1914, the Alliance backed Germany, and by 1916 no candidate could be seen taking money either from brewers, almost all of German ancestry, or from the Alliance. Wets lost the 1916 election, and Wheeler pounced. Once the United States declared war on Germany in April 1917, Congress imposed temporary wartime prohibition to prevent food shortages and passed the Eighteenth Amendment. Ratified in little more than a year, the amendment enjoyed popular support.

When prohibition arrived in 1920, some Americans stopped drinking, and consumption of alcohol during the early twenties may have dropped by two-thirds. Alcohol, however, did not disappear. By the mid-1920s, bootlegging gangsters such as Chicago's Al Capone had accumulated fabulous untaxed wealth. Gang violence turned many Americans against prohibition. Prohibition changed where and how alcohol was consumed. The all-male saloon, notorious for fights, prostitutes, and vote-buying, gave way to the speakeasy, which attracted both men and women. Admission required a pass, a code word, or an introduction from a trusted customer. Police were paid to look the other way. Raids from the federal Prohibition Bureau, however, could cause trouble. Harlem residents held rent parties, where strangers paid to eat, drink, and dance; the tenant earned enough to pay the rent. Many people drank liquor supplied by the bellhop in a rented hotel room. The home cocktail party also gained popularity.

In 1924, Al Smith, the wet Irish Catholic governor of New York, ran for president. At the Democratic National Convention in New York, rural dry forces led by the prohibitionist William Jennings Bryan blocked Smith's nomination. Four years later Smith won the nomination and promised to modify prohibition to allow beer. Southern evangelicals crusaded against Smith as a wet urban Catholic. Five southern states bolted the Democratic Party, and Herbert Hoover, who ran on the promise of better enforcement, easily won the election.

Even before prohibition went into effect, opponents organized for repeal. In 1918, wealthy business executives founded the Association Against the Prohibition Amendment, which aimed to replace high income taxes on the rich with alcohol taxes. More important was Pauline Sabin, an heiress who despised the hypocrisy and criminality surrounding prohibition. In 1929, she founded the Women's Organization for National Prohibition Reform. Arguing on radio, in public appearances, and in pamphlets, Sabin gave wet politicians the cover they needed to confront the WCTU. By 1932, Sabin, a lifelong Republican, decided to back a wet presidential candidate regardless of party.

That candidate turned out to be Governor Franklin Delano Roosevelt of New York. Roosevelt had long waffled on prohibition, at least in part because his wife, Eleanor, was dry. When Roosevelt accepted the Democratic nomination in 1932, he endorsed repeal. Governments at all levels needed alcohol taxes to fight the Great Depression. Congress sent the Twenty-First Amendment repealing the Eighteenth Amendment to the states in early 1933, and a month after Roosevelt's inauguration, legal beer flowed. Tax collection started immediately. In 1933, John D. Rockefeller Jr., a former dry, urged states to restrict alcohol sales. He opposed tied houses, which was the practice before prohibition whereby brewers and distillers had owned saloons, because powerful brewers had used their numerous outlets to control much of American politics.

In 1933, a strong control system replaced prohibition, and since then state governments have limited sales, banned tied houses, imposed high alcohol taxes, and punished alcohol abusers, particularly drunk drivers. Alcohol consumption was low in the 1930s but grew during World War II. The war generation remained heavy drinkers, as were the oldest baby boomers. Per capita consumption peaked in 1980. In the 1980s, Mothers Against Drunk Driving successfully lobbied to raise the legal drinking age to twenty-one. The health movement, fetal alcohol syndrome, and federal policies led to declining consumption until the late 1990s. Since 2000, alcohol consumption has increased as millennials have discovered hard liquor.

Rising and falling patterns of alcohol consumption have been a recurrent feature throughout American history. When alcohol use is low, society shows little interest, which leads to higher use and greater abuse. The increased abuse then leads to tighter restrictions and declining use and abuse. So the cycles have come

5

and gone. National prohibition, however, was a unique and peculiar response to high consumption that bordered on hysteria. Prohibition demonstrated that democracy does not always produce wise public policy, but democratic means were also used to repeal the ban. Democracies make mistakes but are capable of self-correction.

Chapter 1
Drinking and temperance

The earliest European immigrants to the thirteen colonies that
became the United States were hearty drinkers. That fact is not
surprising, since Europe, more than any other continent,
embraced heavy alcohol consumption. Intoxicating beverages have
always been less important in Africa, Asia, and among native
inhabitants in North and South America. In 1607, the Virginia
adventurers brought as much alcohol as they could on their
founding voyage. The settlers subsequently produced corn (maize)
beer and imported rum from the West Indies. Virginians quickly
developed a reputation for hearty drinking. In the early 1700s, the
diarist William Byrd recorded meetings of the Governor's Council
that ended with some members passed out drunk on the floor.
Such was governance in early America. On election days,
candidates were expected to treat voters to free alcohol. In 1755,
when George Washington ran for the Virginia House of Burgesses,
the colonial legislature, he neglected to offer the customary liquor,
and the voters declined to elect him. Three years later,
Washington provided 144 gallons of rum, punch, wine, hard cider,
and beer. He won with 307 votes. Each vote cost almost half a
gallon of alcohol.

Although New Englanders also drank a lot, they, unlike
Virginians, frowned upon public drunkenness. Housewives did
their own brewing, but because the beer they made was low in

alcohol content, it did not keep long and spoiled rapidly. Stronger drink in the form of rum was imported from the West Indies. Rum was distilled from molasses, which was made from sugar cane. Considerable molasses was imported as a sweetener, and some was distilled into rum in New England. Although most rum was consumed locally, it also played a role in international trade. It was shipped to Africa, traded for slaves, and then slaves were traded in the West Indies for molasses, which went to New England to be distilled into more rum. During the 1700s, the Brown family of Rhode Island, later benefactors of Brown University, became the wealthiest and most powerful rum distillers in North America. They imported huge quantities of molasses at a low price, and their large stills had an economy of scale that small-scale producers could not hope to achieve.

By the time of the Revolution, Americans were among the world's heartiest topers. Indeed, much revolutionary activity took place in taverns, whether it was John Hancock and the "Indians" planning the Boston Tea Party, Thomas Jefferson penning and revising the Declaration of Independence in the back room of a Philadelphia drinking house, or recruiting sergeants buying drinks in a public house to entice recruits into the Continental Army. Many a bleary-eyed lad discovered the next morning that he had enlisted while under the influence. Americans imbibed a lot of rum, some beer, and considerable hard cider in areas where apple trees flourished. The British, however, blockaded the colonies during the war, and access to rum was lost. Americans began to distill whiskey from corn instead. Improved distilling technology for small-batch stills had been brought to the colonies when Scottish, Scots-Irish, and Irish immigrants began arriving in large numbers during the 1760s.

After the Revolution, whiskey made from corn and rye became the country's patriotic drink. The distiller Harrison Hall asked, "Why should not our countrymen have a national beverage?" Rum importers or distillers who had to pay duties on molasses or rum that they brought in could not compete in price with the domestic product. In 1791, the federal government tried to level the playing field with a whiskey tax, but western farmers largely defied the law, which led to the Whiskey Rebellion in western Pennsylvania in 1794. Even after this uprising was crushed, the tax was evaded until it was repealed in 1802. American whiskey was usually 50 percent alcohol; not aged; colorless; cheaper than coffee, tea, milk, or beer; and safer than water, since alcohol killed germs. Americans took their whiskey mixed with water. If sugar or lemons were available, they might add a little of each, but such additives were a luxury. Americans drank whiskey morning, noon, and night. All meals were washed down with whiskey. At 11:00 am and in mid-afternoon they took a whiskey break.

Slaves could not drink legally, and they had less access to alcohol than whites did. Slaves, however, often bartered fish or fresh produce for small amounts of alcohol, and many planters gave slaves huge quantities of whiskey to celebrate the New Year by staying drunk for several days. Native Americans traded beaver skins for whiskey. The Indians, who learned about distilled spirits from the Europeans, amazed white Americans by the huge quantities of whiskey that they consumed. Tribes lacked cultural inhibitions against overconsumption, and a few Indians literally drank themselves to death. White Americans, however, drank the most whiskey. Children drank little, although they sometimes finished off a parental glass, especially if there was sugar at the bottom. Taking considerably less whiskey than men, women probably consumed about 15 percent of the total amount. In addition, respectable women neither drank in taverns nor showed drunkenness. By the 1820s, the typical adult white American male consumed nearly a half pint of whiskey a day. This is about three times the present consumption rate. Because they sipped whiskey with meals all day long, they were rarely drunk, but they were often buzzed.

As whiskey consumption rose after the American Revolution, it attracted attention. Medical doctors were among the first to notice the increase. More patients were having the shakes from involuntary withdrawal from alcohol, delirium tremens nightmares and psychoses were on the rise, and solo drinking of massive quantities in binges that ended with the drinker passing out became a new drinking pattern. Doctors such as Benjamin Rush, a signer of the Declaration of Independence and onetime chief physician of the Continental Army, who had first warned against the overuse of whiskey and other distilled spirits during the Revolution, became alarmed. Experts recognized that over time, drinkers needed to increase their use of alcohol to gain the same sense of euphoric satisfaction from drinking. Down that road was chronic drunkenness or what would later be called alcoholism. Medical schools included warnings to students, but most physicians in the early 1800s believed that alcohol was an important medicine. Physicians especially favored laudanum, which was opium dissolved in alcohol. Laudanum calmed the nerves and miraculously ended the craving for alcohol. Children's nurses used laudanum to quiet babies.

To Rush, the issue was not just about health. He published many newspaper articles and pamphlets hostile to distilled spirits. His best-known work, *An Inquiry into the Effects of Spirituous Liquors* (1784), went through at least twenty-one editions and had sold 170,000 copies by 1850. The Philadelphia doctor argued that democracy would be perverted and ultimately destroyed if voters were drunken sots. Public safety in a republic required an electorate capable of wise judgment about political matters. Drunkenness made for bad voters. Rush and others also worried about how distilled spirits damaged society in terms of crime, poverty, and family violence. Many serious crimes, including murder, were committed under the influence of alcohol. The unemployed or unemployable drunkard abandoned his family so that the wife and children sometimes faced starvation while the husband and father debauched himself. Liquor use was often associated with gambling and prostitution, which brought financial ruin and sexually transmitted diseases. Drunkenness also led to wife beating and child abuse. To many Americans, it appeared that the United States could not be a successful republic unless alcoholic passions were curbed.

The generation born during the Revolution that came of age around 1800 was particularly drawn to whiskey. Consumption skyrocketed due to low price and widespread availability. After Americans settled in Kentucky and Ohio, fertile corn-growing areas, a corn surplus developed. Western farmers had no practical way to ship this local glut to market as corn, but they could and did distill spirits and export it to the East. The price of whiskey dropped to 25 cents per gallon. The federal government had stopped taxing whiskey with the repeal of the whiskey tax in 1802, but imported molasses and rum continued to be taxed. Not surprisingly, in 1810, the third most important industry in the United States was making distilled spirits, which accounted for 10 percent of the nation's manufacturing sector. Low price and ready availability stimulated whiskey consumption. Cities and counties required retailers to buy licenses, but licenses were mainly a source of revenue rather than a way to limit sales, and most governments issued as many licenses as there were applicants. No state governments licensed, taxed, or otherwise controlled alcohol.

Problems associated with heavy drinking produced a public reaction. Reformers then created the *temperance movement*. In 1812 a group of Congregational clergy associated with Andover Seminary, prominent business leaders from Boston, and a handful of physicians founded the Massachusetts Society for the Suppression of Intemperance. For the next twenty years these elite reformers met once a year and issued an annual pamphlet lamenting the increase of whiskey consumption and abuse in the United States. The organization did not oppose all alcohol and in fact served wine at its meetings. The group had little impact on public opinion, as suggested by the awkward name, but the

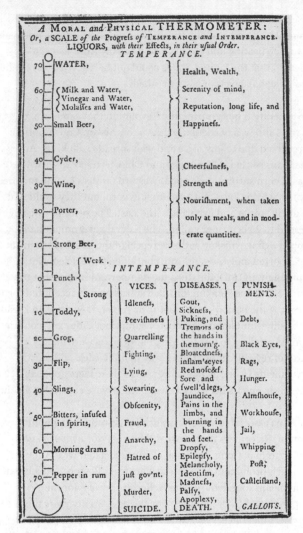

Prohibition

1. According to Dr. Benjamin Rush's popular temperance thermometer, abstinence brought happiness, health, and life, while distilled spirits led to misery, illness, and death.

concerned New England clergy, who read the pamphlets, noticed the growth of alcohol problems inside their own congregations, and they began to preach against overuse of distilled spirits. These ministers did not object to beer, cider, or wine, which was rarely used in America, and they even accepted whiskey either as a medication or as a beverage, if the liquor was sufficiently watered down when it was consumed. They called their campaign to reduce consumption of distilled spirits and eliminate public drunkenness the temperance movement.

Other Protestant preachers took up the cause. These included Quakers and Methodists, two denominations that had turned against alcohol before the American Revolution, as well as growing numbers of southern Baptists and western frontier evangelicals of many new denominations. An upsurge in evangelical Protestant religion began around 1800 on the frontier in Kentucky, Tennessee, and North Carolina and quickly spread north into Indiana and Illinois. Over two decades, these Christian revivals, which later were called the Second Great Awakening, eventually flowed back into the Southeast, upstate New York, and New England. By the 1820s, evangelical Protestantism surged throughout the country. The South witnessed the rise of Methodists and Baptists, Methodism became the most popular denomination in most states, and within another decade or so many new groups, such as the Church of Christ, Disciples of Christ, Seventh-day Adventists, and Church of Jesus Christ of Latter-day Saints, were established.

The religious revivals and the emerging temperance movement were strongly connected. This tie had started with the earliest gatherings in Kentucky. Although the revivals attracted entire families and both whites and blacks, preachers noticed that women were in the majority. Often, women insisted on attending, and husbands drove their wives to the meeting in wagons and then left for the woods to drink while women and children sang hymns and listened to sermons. These men often got drunk and occasionally stumbled into the revival meetings to raise hell. The preachers were not amused. Peter Cartwright, a Methodist in Illinois, picked up a burning log from the campfire and hurled it at several drunkards. As the fiery object fell, Cartwright shouted that hellfire was descending upon the wicked. Ministers denounced the Demon Rum. "The devil," declared the Reverend Huntington Lyman, "had an efficient hand in establishing, perfecting, and sustaining the present system of making drunkards."

Large numbers of evangelical churches required their members to abstain from hard liquor. "We may set it down as a probable sign of a false conversion," advised one preacher, "if he allows himself to *taste a single drop*." Giving up whiskey enabled the convert to prove sincerity and make a life-altering change that would carry over into family and religious life. The revivals that peaked during the 1820s marked the first great effort to control alcohol use in America. During the 1830s, many evangelicals redefined *temperance*. The word no longer meant abstinence from hard liquor. Now churches required members to take the *teetotal pledge*, that is, to abstain from all alcoholic beverages. This shift had both philosophical and practical roots. It was hard to justify calling for abstinence only from hard liquor. Could not all forms of alcohol be pernicious? Then, too, the promise to drink only beer, cider, or wine clashed with the temptation to drink whiskey in a society where whiskey was pervasive. John Tappan wrote, "Daily experience convinces us that we must include all intoxicating drinks in our pledge, or the excepted drinks will perpetuate drunkenness thro' all coming generations."

Before 1830, anti-liquor forces had not opposed consumption of wine because it was so expensive and rare that only a few wealthy people drank it, and they did so in the privacy of the home. Wine had no association with public drunkenness or alcoholism. Then, too, Saint Paul had advised, "Use a little wine for thy stomach's sake," and the Bible called for wine in the communion sacrament.

During the 1830s, evangelicals reinterpreted the Bible and persuaded themselves (if not Episcopalians, Catholics, and Jews) that the wine in the Bible was the unfermented juice of the grape, that is, grape juice. New bottling techniques eventually appeared that made year-round grape juice possible for religious purposes.

Temperance advocates also argued that the rich had to sacrifice wine, which was harmless, to get the poor to give up whiskey, which was harmful. A similar plea was made concerning hard apple cider. Widely used only in rural America, this drink caused little trouble, but farmers were told to abandon cider so that Americans addicted to whiskey would stop consumption. Before the Revolution, housewives had brewed a mild beer that spoiled in two or three days; after 1800, cheap whiskey that did not spoil had replaced this rural beer. In the 1820s, when the country was overwhelmingly rural, there were few beer drinkers, but they were also expected to quit their beverage of choice in order to rid the nation of whiskey.

Dry propaganda flooded the country. Lyman Beecher, a prominent evangelical Protestant minister and the father of Harriet Beecher Stowe, author of *Uncle Tom's Cabin*, issued *Six Sermons on Intemperance* (1826). That same year the American Temperance Society began to publish anti-liquor tracts, as did the successor American Temperance Union in 1836. Edward Delavan, a former wine merchant converted to teetotalism, ran a major anti-liquor press in Albany, New York. He once mailed a broadside to every household in New York State, and in the 1840s, he supplied every schoolroom in New York with a colored drawing illustrating the diseased state of a drunkard's stomach. In 1851, the American Tract Society reported that it had circulated nearly five million temperance pamphlets. Dry advocates, or those who promoted consuming no alcohol of any kind, produced lectures, poetry, songs, novels, and plays. John B. Gough, a self-styled reformed drunkard, made a fortune on the lecture circuit telling anti-liquor stories in which he acted out the part of a drunkard.

Timothy S. Arthur's best-selling novel, *Ten Nights in a Bar-Room* (1854), was quickly turned into a hit stage production.

Temperance forces organized local societies throughout the country, although most were concentrated in smaller cities in the Northeast that were experiencing rapid economic growth brought by early industrialization. In 1831, the American Temperance Society reported 2,700 local groups with 170,000 members; three years later, there were 7,000 groups with 1,250,000 members, which was close to 10 percent of the total population. Women made up 35 to 60 percent of the members of the local societies, and they were usually among the most enthusiastic supporters. Societies enabled members to meet other abstainers, employers, employees, or customers. In boom towns along the Erie Canal such as Rochester, New York, employers often hired new employees through evangelical church or temperance society connections, and social events included dry picnics, concerts, and public lectures. Because taverns had often been the only large venues in a small community, temperance groups built meeting halls to house events where alcohol would not be served. Reform organizations and political parties used these halls. Women participated as equals in these activities.

Anti-liquor forces lobbied elected officials, many of whom were heavy drinkers, for restrictions against alcohol sales or better enforcement of existing laws. Washington, DC, was awash in saloons and soggy boarding houses, but drys were particularly appalled that alcohol was sold in the basement cafe of the US Capitol, where members drank, told stories, and swapped votes. Lewis Cass, a Michigan Democrat who ran for president in 1848, converted to the dry cause. In 1832, as secretary of war, he had abolished the Army spirits ration, and a year later he became the founding president of the Congressional Temperance Society. There was a need. Writing privately to a friend, Senator Henry Wise of Virginia noted that frequently among his legislative colleagues "members [were] too drunk for the decency of a tavern bar-room." The society's meetings drew many members, who eagerly joined to placate their dry constituents. Even the frequently drunk Daniel Webster, who claimed that his best speeches were all given while he was well oiled, astonished colleagues by attending one temperance meeting. In 1837, Congress bowed to dry pressure and banned liquor sales in the basement cafe, but the reform did not last, and the Congressional Temperance Society faded into insignificance during the mid-1840s.

Between 1825 and 1850, the amount of alcohol consumed per person in the United States dropped by half. This was a remarkable shift in a short period of time. The evangelical revivals and the temperance movement had much to do with this change. It was not so much that Americans drank half as much alcohol. Rather, a large number, approaching 50 percent in many small towns where the evangelical movement had been especially strong, had simply stopped drinking at all. The use of alcohol became socially unacceptable, particularly in middle-class circles in small towns. Middle-class employers refused to employ anyone who drank. To advance in business or society, a person found it necessary to abstain. Advice books and novels, which were beginning to circulate among the middle class, told young women not to marry any man who drank. In New York State in 1839, a reliable estimate held that a majority of the physicians and 85 percent of the Protestant clergy had ceased to use any alcohol.

For a variety of reasons, the vast majority of residents of America's large cities never embraced the temperance movement. Cities were by definition diverse. Seaports, in particular, had hard-drinking residents and visitors, including sailors, from all parts of the world. Nor had the revivals that had started on the frontier ever caught on in the great cities. Evangelical Protestants denounced restaurants, theaters, and musical performances as ungodly frivolities, but many city residents enjoyed these urban delights. Almost all public places in cities sold alcohol.

Although massive Irish Catholic immigration did not begin until the 1840s, a number of Irish Catholics had already migrated to the largest cities, such as New York. Episcopalians, Catholics, and Jews approved of the use of alcohol. The Catholic Church, however, opposed public drunkenness, and the Irish priest Father Theobald Mathew visited America's great cities to urge Catholics to abstain voluntarily from alcohol as a personal commitment to reduce public drunkenness. In any case, New York City remained wet, and when drys in the state legislature in 1846 required every town in New York State to vote on local option liquor licenses, the city was exempted from the vote, since it was understood that the city would vote overwhelmingly wet. Of 856 townships and cities that held elections, 728 voted dry.

The early Industrial Revolution played a role in the temperance movement as well. To middle-class Americans who lived in small towns, getting ahead financially and socially was a real possibility in the emerging market economy of the mid-1800s. To do so, a person needed education, a good reputation, and access to credit. When the evangelical reformer Lewis Tappan set up his credit rating agency, the forerunner of Dun and Bradstreet, in 1841, the firm evaluated business prospects as to their creditworthiness partly on the basis of the owners' drinking habits. Teetotalers, mostly evangelicals, were rated the highest, and anyone with an interest in the liquor industry was all but eliminated as a borrower. By the 1830s, colleges no longer served alcohol on campus, and students, faculty, or staff who drank were dismissed. Temperance forces established dry steamboat lines, dry hotels, and dry restaurants. The same reformers who opposed liquor often backed the abolition of slavery and women's rights. All these reforms were rooted in the belief in the dignity of the individual soul. White southerners became suspicious of the ties between temperance and abolition, and before 1860 the temperance movement was weaker in the South than in the North, although some southern churches demanded that members take the pledge.

Alternative beverages also changed drinking habits. Amid flourishing trade, the United States began to import significant quantities of coffee, which largely replaced whiskey. The old-fashioned whiskey break became the coffee break. Coffee was safer to drink around machinery, which began to appear in the emerging industrial age. To a lesser extent, tea and cocoa imports also increased, although those items were rarely consumed by anyone outside the urban middle class. Governments, strongly supported by dry forces, built public water supply systems in major cities. Philadelphia constructed the Fairmont Works, and in 1842, New York City opened the Croton Aqueduct, which piped in pure water from upstate. The city had long suffered from brackish wells that were easily susceptible to contamination from nearby outhouses. Croton water was free to every resident who hooked up, and the city installed numerous public water fountains.

During the 1820s and early 1830s, evangelicals were convinced that their temperance crusade would dry out the United States in a short time as drinkers saw the light and renounced the Demon Rum. Children signed the teetotal pledge, and dry forces sponsored parades and cold water picnics. Abolitionists at the same time hoped that southern slaveholders would voluntarily relinquish their slaves. Neither anti-liquor nor anti-slavery forces succeeded, and by the late 1830s, both groups were disillusioned. At the time, reformers saw alcohol as the greater problem: Drinking took place throughout the country, while slavery was relegated to the South. Some evangelicals also believed that alcohol sent drinkers to hell. In contrast, slavery merely harmed the body temporarily. Reformers could also see that curbing liquor, at least in northern states where evangelicals were strong, appeared to be easier politically than ending slavery. To force drinkers to give up alcohol, drys shifted from voluntary abstinence to using state coercive power.

Massachusetts passed the first coercive law in 1838. To prevent saloons from selling liquor by the drink, the law provided that distilled spirits could be sold only in a minimum of fifteen gallons, the size of a small barrel. To gain passage of the law, legislators excluded beer, cider, or wine. In theory, respectable middle-class or farm families could store hard liquor for medicinal or household purposes, but the tavern or saloon that sold single glasses to the urban working class would disappear. The statute failed to work the way that its advocates intended. One tavern keeper owned a blind pig, and for a small sum, customers could see it. A free drink awaited in the room beyond the pig. This is the origin of the expression "blind pig" to describe an illegal drinking establishment. The ineffective law was repealed in 1842.

The anti-liquor movement took a new turn in 1840, when six working-class drunkards met in the back of a Baltimore tavern and resolved to stop drinking. To do so, they formed the Washingtonian Society, a self-help group. Members met two or three times a week to share personal experiences. Naming the group in honor of George Washington, they said that, like Washington, they were first—in their case, the first drunkards to reform. The idea spread rapidly, and by 1847 there were 600,000 members. At first, middle-class evangelicals were skeptical about the Washingtonians, but they were welcomed as allies in the late 1840s. In 1842, the Sons of Temperance emerged as another self-help group. They claimed 220,000 members nationally by 1849. Unlike the Washingtonians, the mostly middle-class Sons accepted members who were not self-confessed drunkards. Both groups had women's auxiliaries. In 1851, the Independent Order of Good Templars (IOGT) was founded at Utica, New York. A dry lodge, the IOGT was, unlike the Freemasons, pledged to personal abstinence and prohibition. Women and men were accepted as equals. After the Civil War, the IOGT grew to seven million members.

In the 1840s, many dry Americans no longer wished to live in communities where liquor attracted derelicts and criminals, and where drunkards beat or starved their wives and children. To

PARALLEL

BETWEEN

INTEMPERANCE

AND THE

SLAVE-TRADE.

BY HEMAN HUMPHREY, D. D.

PRESIDENT OF AMHERST COLLEGE, MASSACHUSETTS.

"Drag me, bound and bleeding, if you will, from my blazing habitation—but—O bind me not to a rack, where I can neither live nor die under the torture."—*P.* 10.

PUBLISHED BY JOHN P. HAVEN,

No. 142 *Nassau-street.*

Price $1 75 per hundred. $15 per thousand.

2. The Reverend Heman Humphrey, president of Amherst College, linked the anti-liquor and anti-slavery causes in this 1828 tract. Many Northern reformers favored both movements.

21

create dry islands within the wet sea, temperance supporters turned to local option licensing. For the first time, anti-liquor forces began to use government power to stop alcohol consumption by imposing *prohibition*. Under this system, once the state passed a proper enabling statute, voters in a city, county, or other local area could ban all liquor sales, and local officials would then refuse to grant any liquor licenses. Going back to medieval England and continuing into colonial America, licenses had always been required to sell alcohol. Partly, the license system raised revenue, but it also guaranteed that officials monitored who was selling liquor. Alcohol was connected to gambling and prostitution, which were far less acceptable to the public than alcohol.

Local option licensing, however, brought problems. Unless a city had a strong tax base, it often needed the license fees. Also, liquor sales might continue on an unlicensed basis if licenses were not available. Under those conditions, city officials not only lost revenue but also lacked the leverage to force saloons to act responsibly or lose their licenses. Finally, many residents lived close to a wet jurisdiction. As soon as a locality voted itself dry, a saloon or store that sold alcohol might pop up just across the border. The dry town lost license fees but suffered from liquor imported from outside the town limits.

Mayor Neal Dow of Portland, Maine, found a solution. Dow, a businessman and teetotaler of Quaker background, loathed alcohol. In 1851, he persuaded the legislature to pass the nation's first statewide prohibition law, which became known as the Maine Law. Dry jurisdictions would be safe from neighboring wet areas, except in a narrow strip along the state border. Dow then campaigned for similar laws in other states. Evangelicals lobbied for statewide prohibition laws in the 1850s. From 1851 to 1855, eleven states passed such laws. The six states of New England headed the list, joined by New York, Michigan, Indiana, Iowa, and Delaware. All contained large numbers of evangelicals, and all were in the North, except Delaware, which did, however, contain a lot of dry Methodists.

None of these laws, including Maine's, lasted, and most were gone by 1865. In Delaware, Indiana, Massachusetts, New York, and Rhode Island, state supreme courts invalidated anti-liquor laws, sometimes finding legal technicalities, sometimes disapproving of popular votes to enact legislation, or sometimes citing personal liberty, an argument embraced by wet Democrats. Legally valid statutes sometimes replaced the flawed ones. In Connecticut, New York, and Wisconsin, governors vetoed prohibition statutes; in Connecticut and New York, new governors signed follow-up laws. But German lovers of lager beer blocked voter approval of a prohibition law in Pennsylvania in 1854.

The alcohol issue was entangled in rising immigration. More than two million Irish and German migrants flooded into the United States during the 1840s and 1850s. Both countries of origin had heavy drinking cultures. The Irish favored whiskey, which they claimed to have invented; indeed, the word *whiskey* was corrupted from an Irish word, *usquebaugh*. Germans were identified with lager beer, a type of lightly colored and mildly alcoholic German beer that had to be aged (or lagered) before it was ready to drink. By 1860, Irish and German immigrants were almost 10 percent of the American population. Their influence, however, was much greater because they settled heavily in America's economically booming cities. In some cities, immigrants and their American-born children were a majority. The Irish, rarely having the money to move inland, favored the eastern seaports of Boston, New York, Philadelphia, and Baltimore, while the Germans were concentrated in the Midwest in Cincinnati, Chicago, St. Louis, and especially Milwaukee. In 1860, a majority of the residents of Milwaukee were of German ancestry. Germans also acquired farms in Wisconsin, Illinois, Iowa, and Missouri. Few Irish or German immigrants settled in the South because they did not want to compete for jobs with low-cost slave labor.

Much of Irish immigrant culture revolved around the saloon where men drank, talked politics, and conducted business deals. The saloonkeepers, mostly Irish immigrants, arranged jobs, lent money, passed along messages, and advised about voting. The saloon was often the voting place, and city political machines frequently provided chits that voters could cash for a free drink after they had cast their ballots. Many saloonkeepers became city aldermen. The Germans enjoyed saloons, too, but they also had beer gardens, often located on the edge of town, where entire families gathered, especially on Sundays, to sing songs, to play sports, to eat bratwurst and other German foods, and to drink lager beer. While almost all the Irish immigrants were Roman Catholics, a tiny group in the United States before 1840, the Germans were split between Catholics and Lutherans. Unlike America's evangelical Protestants, neither religious group regarded abstinence from alcohol as a sign of holiness. Evangelicals disliked Catholicism, abhorred Irish saloonkeepers involved in politics, and despised Germans who celebrated Sundays with drinking festivities that included children.

Both the local option and statewide prohibition laws of the 1850s were attempts by evangelicals to impose on society their own practices, including the quiet family Sabbath when all businesses were shuttered. Evangelicals stopped Sunday mail delivery, tried to prohibit commercial travel on Sunday, and frequently passed local ordinances that banned the sale of alcohol on the Sabbath. These ideas clashed with the practices of many immigrants, who were expected to conform to the will of the majority. The evangelical position was ironic, because forty years earlier American drinking habits would have resembled those of the new arrivals. To the immigrants, the demand was absurd. They had no intention of giving up traditions that enabled them to keep in touch with each other and that served as reminders of their own culture. On Sunday, the front door of the saloon might be locked and the blinds drawn, but those who knocked at a side door would be admitted. Some immigrants served alcohol in private homes and denied that these were saloons, although they were in fact substituting for saloons. Beer gardens sometimes compromised by delaying the opening until Sunday afternoon, or they paid off government officials to look the other way.

In the 1850s, a bitter political fight took place in Ohio, which had many evangelicals, especially in the northeast part of the state where settlers from New England predominated. Cincinnati, on the other hand, became a great German immigrant city where beer flowed freely. The Whig Party, heavily composed of evangelicals, fell apart over the demand to curtail alcohol sales in Cincinnati and especially to close beer gardens on Sunday. The Know-Nothings in Cincinnati rose to prominence in the mid-1850s to express this anti-liquor backlash, but professional politicians, who could count votes, steered clear, because any party that attacked immigrant drinking could not win statewide elections. Smart politicians ignored the liquor question to create the Republican Party as a coalition of evangelicals and German immigrants from Cincinnati who all abhorred slavery.

The statewide laws in the 1850s suffered from the inability of the drafters to create any viable system of enforcement. Some drys naively believed that if the law were passed, it would be honored, but this proved to be untrue in large cities, mining districts, seaports, or logging areas with large numbers of single young men. Other drys were more cynical. They knew the state laws would not be enforced; however, their main concern was not to stop individual drinkers but the alcohol industry. By making the industry illegal, everyone connected to it could be made odious. This would force respectable people out of the liquor business. Given the lack of police forces and the general understanding that police power was limited in the 1850s, these laws simply could not be enforced. There was neither the political will nor the governmental resources to back the law. By 1860, attention had swung from alcohol to slavery, and most statewide dry laws had been abandoned or were no longer enforced.

During the Civil War, the federal government badly needed new revenue. A wartime income tax proved difficult to collect and easy to evade, and Congress repealed it as soon as the war ended, but high alcohol taxes imposed in 1862 were retained. Recognizing the need for wartime revenue, temperance forces supported these taxes on the grounds that higher prices would discourage consumption. Abraham Lincoln had been active in the temperance movement early in life; he persuaded Congress to impose a far higher tax on whiskey than on beer. No longer would a glass of whiskey cost the same or even less than a glass of beer. Little wine was drunk at this time, but its rate of taxation was between the taxes levied on beer and whiskey. The distillers resisted the tax, and after the war they were caught bribing government inspectors to allow untaxed liquor to be withdrawn from storage. Their greed, dishonesty, and lack of wartime patriotism ruined the distillers' reputations. The brewers, mostly German immigrants, cheerfully paid the beer tax. The major brewers created the United States Brewers' Association to lobby for a tax law that did not unduly burden the industry; they were also astute enough to know that if the government permanently taxed beer, it would never be outlawed.

The Civil War affected alcohol consumption in one other way: German immigrants in the Union army introduced other soldiers to lager beer. Officers preferred that soldiers drink mildly alcoholic beer rather than whiskey, which seemed to lead to arguments and fights. Whiskey, however, was used medicinally to treat war wounds. One-quarter of Union army soldiers were immigrants, mostly from Ireland and Germany, and much anti-immigrant sentiment disappeared in the aftermath of this military service. The veterans' association, the Grand Army of the Republic, was a cross-class and multiethnic organization that offered social, economic, and political advancement to all veterans regardless of place of birth. After the war, many veterans continued to drink, and drinking may have increased in response to painful wounds that did not heal properly, psychological problems, and unemployment. In the United States as a whole, consumption shifted gradually from whiskey to beer. The low cost of beer, continuing German immigration, and urbanization all played a role in this change.

Chapter 2
The dry crusade

Dio Lewis, a homeopathic physician and itinerant lecturer, made his living by speaking in small towns. In December 1873 he gave a series of talks in Hillsboro, Ohio, denouncing the Demon Rum. The effect on the evangelical Protestant women who attended his presentations was electrifying. Looking around Hillsboro, they saw the town's many raunchy saloons through new eyes, and they decided to act. Led by the wives and daughters of leading citizens, dozens of women descended upon one saloon, entered this all-male sanctuary, and proceeded to pray on their knees and sing hymns. They said they would leave as soon as the seller agreed to close the business. Several saloonkeepers quickly capitulated, which put more pressure on the others to conform. Within a short time, Hillsboro went dry.

News of the Hillsboro campaign spread in the newspapers, including the temperance press, and evangelical women in other small towns in Ohio and western upstate New York also took direct action. Thus was born the Women's Crusade of 1873–1874. Middle-class women dried up dozens of small towns, but when anti-liquor reformers in larger towns led similar movements, they met defiance and resistance. In big cities the reaction was fierce. In Cincinnati, praying women were locked out of the saloons, which admitted only regular customers, and a few saloonkeepers' wives located in upstairs apartments dumped the contents of chamber pots upon the heads of the protesters. Sometimes they were drenched with stale beer. Although the demonstrations were mostly peaceful, rocks occasionally broke barroom windows, and sellers learned to shutter their windows before the crusaders arrived. This anti-liquor crusade accompanied the economic crash of 1873, which produced a depression that lasted until the end of the decade.

In November 1874, dozens of middle-class women, many of them veterans of the Women's Crusade, met in Cleveland, Ohio, to found the Woman's Christian Temperance Union (WCTU). They

3. Well-dressed protesters gathered at the rear of a saloon in Mount Vernon, Ohio, during the 1873–1874 Women's Crusade.

elected Annie Wittenmyer of Philadelphia the first president. The new organization chartered local groups that planned their own dry campaigns according to what locals considered to be most beneficial in their own communities. The national organization provided speakers, issued a publication, later called the *Union Signal*, advised how to set up a society, and acted as a clearinghouse for information. The group used *woman* instead of *women* in its title to indicate that it promoted a feminine or feminist sensibility and was not just an organization composed of women. The WCTU was ecumenical among Christians, although it had little appeal beyond evangelicals, and ties to the Methodist Church were strong. The WCTU enabled women to participate in their communities at a time when women could not vote.

Frances Willard was elected the corresponding secretary at the first national meeting. She had already shown remarkable leadership in incorporating a women's college into Northwestern University. Named the school's first woman dean, she was a tireless fundraiser. In 1879, Willard became the president of the WCTU, a position that she held until her death in 1898. She steered the organization in new directions. Under the brilliant and insightful slogan "Home Protection," Willard pushed to ban not only alcohol but also gambling, tobacco, opium, pornography, and prostitution. Critical of urban poverty and juvenile delinquency, the WCTU favored free kindergartens and prison reform. To the public, Willard and the WCTU represented the women's sphere, a theory of separate female development popular in the United States in the late 1800s. Willard had a broader vision: When women lobbied legislators, wrote letters, held meetings, and organized petitions, they were preparing for voting and citizenship.

In another initiative, the WCTU introduced the program of Scientific Temperance into the public school curriculum. Mary Hunt headed a WCTU bureau that supplied lecturers, provided school materials, trained teachers to instruct students against using liquor, and made certain that textbooks opposed alcohol. Materials presented alcohol as a poison and showed students gruesome photographs and charts about alcoholic deaths. In 1891, thirty-five states required temperance education in public schools. WCTU members interviewed candidates for teaching positions, and school boards were pressured to hire only abstainers. Children educated in the late 1800s were thus inculcated with hostile attitudes against alcohol. That fact helped spur the Progressive Era surge toward prohibition.

Using the motto "Do Everything," WCTU members specialized in whatever reform was closest to their hearts. A committed feminist, Willard pushed women's suffrage, which attracted many women. Under Willard, the WCTU grew to become the largest women's organization in the United States with 200,000 members in 1890. She also traveled to Europe and in 1891 established the World's WCTU with herself as president. The first global women's organization, the WWCTU coordinated with women's anti-liquor groups in Australia, India, the United Kingdom, Scandinavia, and Germany.

In 1881 and 1883, when Willard toured the South to establish the WCTU there, she found that her own close ties to the Republican Party proved a handicap. Whereas educated, elite women, who were most often local WCTU leaders, were usually Republicans in the North, they were almost always Democrats in the South. Willard accepted that the WCTU in the South supported Democrats, but she was forced to create separate local affiliates for southern African Americans to placate southern whites. The national WCTU always seated black delegates at annual meetings.

Willard gradually grew disenchanted with the Republican Party's unwillingness to embrace prohibition. In 1869, dry extremists irritated with Republicans and Democrats founded the Prohibition Party, and in 1884 they nominated John St. John, former Republican governor of Kansas, for president. He won Willard's backing, but the WCTU declined to follow. St. John won only 1.5 percent of the vote. The Prohibition Party's presidential vote peaked in 1892 with 2.25 percent. As critics noted at the time, Willard's Do Everything policy and her political gyrations weakened the ability of the WCTU either to enact prohibition or to influence the two major parties that were key to political success.

Although southern temperance forces were a minority during the 1870s, they were growing and had ties to leading Baptist and Methodist clergy. Because the southern states were poor and needed schools and roads, dry leaders and elected officials backed high license fees for saloons and grocers who sold alcohol. High fees were supposed to eliminate disreputable sellers. During the 1880s, however, temperance support for high license fees faded, and in 1887 the Tennessee Conference of the Southern Methodist Church declared, "The license system is an evil." Ten years later the Georgia Baptist Convention stated, "The license system is in league with hell and the devil, and must die."

Dry fervor produced an increasing demand in the South for communities to be able to impose local prohibition. Every southern state adopted local option by 1890. Even if the votes were lacking to prohibit alcohol statewide, there might be enough votes to support a ban in a county, in a portion of a county, or in a town. Legislation usually called for voters to decide the issue of licensing in local elections, which brought the liquor question into politics, where the alcohol industry exerted pressure to allow sales. Under local option, evangelicals dried up large geographical areas in the South during the 1890s. Another strategy was to ban alcohol sales near churches, schools, or colleges. In Tennessee, for example, alcohol was banned within four miles of any rural church or school, which more or less made rural Tennessee dry.

One alternative to using local option to ban sales was the Gothenburg System, invented in Sweden, whereby government-run dispensaries sold distilled spirits for home consumption. Profits went to the government instead of the liquor dealer, and personal consumption could be monitored or limited, as the dispensaries kept individual sales records. Although many reformers supported this system, evangelicals who hated the Demon Rum disliked the idea. A few jurisdictions adopted the plan, including Athens, Georgia, in 1891. Two years later Governor Benjamin "Pitchfork Ben" Tillman (D-SC) forced a statewide dispensary system through the legislature to derail prohibition. In addition to considerable revenue, dispensaries created numerous patronage jobs, which Tillman quickly filled with supporters. North Carolina, Alabama, and Virginia allowed local dispensaries, but only South Carolina adopted this plan statewide. The law proved problematic. Local political factions resisted state control, and liquor leaked through employee theft. The system did not satisfy prohibitionists, and South Carolina abolished its dispensaries in 1907.

Anti-liquor radicals wanted state and national prohibition. They were frustrated by the rise of local option in the 1880s and 1890s. "When there is a vigorous public sentiment on any question of morals," a WCTU writer stated, "it is because somebody has taken an advanced position." The trouble with advanced positions is that they cannot, in a democracy, produce political success. In the 1880s, drys forced reluctant legislators to put statewide prohibition on the ballot in sixteen states. Anti-liquor crusaders won only four of these elections, and all four bans were subsequently repealed. When frustrated drys backed the anemic Prohibition Party in 1884, 1888, and 1892, they mostly revealed their own insignificance.

Because the North was richer, government officials in that region had less interest in revenue from high license fees, and because evangelicals were a minority in much of the North, especially places heavily settled by Irish and German immigrants, local option became more important in the North than in the South from the 1870s through the 1890s. By 1900, America had many dry towns and counties, but most of the country remained wet. The only dry states were rural—Kansas, North Dakota, Maine, Vermont, and New Hampshire.

In the 1870s and 1880s, Irish Catholic immigrants and their descendants in certain cities created a significant temperance movement. Upwardly striving middle-class Irish were embarrassed by saloons, drunkenness, and vice. In St. Paul, Minnesota, a heavily Catholic and militantly wet locale, Bishop John Ireland led the Catholic Total Abstinence Union. In the late 1870s, a thousand Irish activists cooperated with the Sons of Temperance and the Good Templars in pledging voluntary abstinence. Ireland and his followers wanted to remake the "drunken Paddy" stereotype. In 1876, 9 percent of St. Paul's Irish Catholics belonged to temperance societies. To Ireland's regret, German Catholics showed no interest in temperance. Germans brewed almost all the city's beer, and in 1887 Germans operated 45 percent of St. Paul's saloons; the Irish had only 9 percent. Local Catholics universally opposed prohibition.

Employers often opposed alcohol in the late 1800s. Paternalistic founders of large corporations took a personal interest in the welfare of their workers, even as their companies exploited labor. George Pullman built his eponymous sleeping cars in the Chicago suburbs in order to establish a factory surrounded by a model dry town. Absenteeism from drunkenness declined. Thomas Edison located his engineering works and lightbulb factory in Menlo Park, New Jersey. The inventor effectively kept saloons away from the site. Later, the fanatically dry Henry Ford moved his auto company from Detroit to suburban Dearborn. Ford workers were not allowed to drink either on or off the job, and company spies checked garbage cans at workers' homes for liquor bottles.

No dry employer opposed the use of alcohol more vigorously than John D. Rockefeller, whose Standard Oil Company monopolized the petroleum industry. Realizing that oil was the key commodity in the machine age, he had cornered the market to become America's first billionaire. Although Rockefeller had practical reasons to oppose alcohol in a refinery, his fanaticism was rooted in his Baptist faith. He really did believe in the Demon Rum. This stupendously wealthy man and his son, John D. Rockefeller Jr., contributed $350,000 to the Anti-Saloon League from 1900 to 1919.

The dry crusade also appealed to some native-born labor leaders, and the railroad brotherhoods required abstinence. Terence Powderly of the Knights of Labor, for instance, favored prohibition. In 1895 he declared, "No workingman ever drank a glass of rum who did not rob his wife and children of the price of it." The Knights excluded liquor dealers from membership, and the heavily German brewery workers union bolted to the new American Federation of Labor over Powderly's anti-liquor stance. Under Samuel Gompers, the AFL avoided controversial social issues.

To evade employer spies, many union locals met in saloons. Workers were allowed to use a back room if they purchased beer. Another source of anxiety about saloons, especially in New York and Chicago in the 1880s and 1890s, came from drinking houses that harbored political radicals, particularly anarchists who had migrated from Germany. Anarchists drank beer, held discussions, and planned strikes or protests, including bombings. These establishments displayed prints of Karl Marx on the wall and stocked radical newspapers such as *Freiheit*. As anarchists, they defied the law to stay open on Sundays.

A lot of the rising hostility to saloons came from growing opposition to illegal gambling and prostitution. Moral purity crusades were strong where large numbers of single young men congregated, which was often the case in immigrant communities. "Alien illiterates rule our cities today," declared Frances Willard. "The saloon is their palace; the toddy stick their scepter." Rough urban working-class male culture enraged middle-class women devoted to family, education, moral improvement, and social uplift. Saloons displayed pictures of female nudes, stank of urine and stale beer, had tobacco spittle on the floor, and sold cigars as well as alcohol. In addition to promoting easy sex, saloons were often the sites of drunken brawls. Their powerful role in politics angered feminists, who knew that saloonkeepers opposed women's suffrage.

While the WCTU tried to civilize the country by closing saloons, drinking houses flourished in the West. Mining towns from Virginia City, Nevada, to Leadville, Colorado, and Bisbee, Arizona, were rife with boisterous miners, rowdy saloons, faro games, and prostitutes. "The entire fabric of the Territory was constructed on liquor," an Arizona pioneer recalled. In 1876, Wild Bill Hickok, a legendary frontier sheriff, was shot while playing poker in a saloon with his back turned unwisely to the door in Deadwood, Dakota Territory. The raunchiness, violence, and romance of the hard-drinking western saloon as an essential element of American life lasted well into the twentieth century. The German composer Kurt Weill and librettist Bertolt Brecht took up the theme in the opera *The Rise and Fall of the City of Mahagonny* (1930), and for two decades Marshal Matt Dillon and Doc Adams hung out at Miss Kitty's saloon in Dodge City on the long-running hit television series *Gunsmoke* (1955–1975).

If cowboys indulged in drunken sprees at the end of the Chisholm Trail, so did the native inhabitants of the Great Plains. Alcohol played a role in buffalo hunts and ghost dances. So liquor on the frontier in the nineteenth century also meant lucrative trade with Native Americans, who were sometimes plied with spirits until they handed over valuable furs, horses, or land. Trade in the white man's firewater dated to colonial times. Indian violence under the influence of liquor led the federal government in 1834 to curb private vending to native peoples on reservations. The statute, however, did not apply off reservations. In 1862 and 1874, Congress enacted new restrictions, but these measures proved ineffective. In 1892, Congress imposed a more robust form of prohibition on Native Americans over whom the federal government exercised guardianship. Reservations became officially dry, although Indians continued to drink. In 1953, Indian prohibition was repealed; today, some tribes continue to ban alcohol sales on their land.

While the temperance forces concentrated on drying out the United States with new legislation, the problem of drunkenness remained. Moral exhortations against drinking had a limited effect on the nation's numerous alcoholics. In 1866, Dr. Leslie Keeley, a Union army surgeon, settled in Dwight, Illinois, about seventy miles south of Chicago. Many of his patients had serious drinking problems, and in 1879 he announced, "Drunkenness is a

4. The all-male clientele of this saloon in the mining town of Central City, Colorado, was typical of frontier watering holes in the 1870s.

disease and I can cure it." A year later, the Keeley Institute opened in Dwight to provide four-week treatments at one of the world's first detoxification centers. Bed rest, excellent meals, and refined conversation were part of the therapy, but so were oral infusions or injections of Keeley's double chloride of gold cure. In the 1880s and 1890s, hundreds of patients arrived at the Keeley Institute each week to begin treatment. By 1896, Keeley had made a fortune by franchising 126 treatment centers in nine countries.

Around 1900, alcohol policy in the United States was contradictory and ambiguous. While most of the country was legally wet, there were many dry localities, although some were only nominally dry. In other words, it was easy to find a drink. A certain amount of naivete prevailed inside the WCTU. Though respectable women neither drank alcohol nor visited saloons, they used tonics, such as Lydia E. Pinkham's Vegetable Compound. Herbal alcohol-infused potions were especially favored for coping with menstrual cycles or menopause. In 1904, the Massachusetts Board of Health tested Pinkham's elixir and found it was 20.6 percent alcohol. Frances Willard herself for a time drank a "medicinal" glass of beer with her daily dinner.

For decades, the main organized opposition to prohibition came from the alcohol industry. As was the case in many other industries after the Civil War, large-scale manufacturers became dominant. In the three decades after 1865, cheap abundant corn and proximity to the Midwest market led distilling to be concentrated in Illinois and Kentucky under the monopoly control of the Distilling Company of America, which was commonly called the Whiskey Trust. German immigrants established nationally important breweries, especially in Milwaukee (Pabst, Schlitz, and Blatz), Cincinnati (Moerlein), and St. Louis (Anheuser-Busch and Lemp). German-style lager beer could not be brewed in hot weather, and Milwaukee's short summer gave it an edge. Its beer was shipped to Chicago and beyond. Busch captured much of the important Texas beer market by becoming the first brewer to use refrigerated railroad cars.

Industrial capitalism in the late 1800s favored the producer over the retailer. Major breweries established tied-house saloons, that is, the brewers owned or financially controlled the saloons, and each saloonkeeper agreed to sell only one brand of beer. The brewer provided the building, furniture, fixtures, and inventory in return for monthly rent. High wholesale prices, which included big producer profits, kept profit margins for the retailer low. Producers franchised far too many outlets in order to deny a market to competitors. A national brewer might locate four or six saloons on a single block to capture foot traffic and keep out rivals. In 1909, brewers owned or controlled 70 percent of the nation's saloons. In New York City and Chicago, 80 percent of saloons were tied houses. These numbers do not count the outlets that the distillers controlled. While this system benefited the producer, it did not help the retailer, who was forced to sell beer at the same low price as the competitors. Some saloonkeepers used musical entertainment or games to attract customers, but the more lucrative way was to offer illegal gambling or prostitution. In one working-class neighborhood in Chicago, prostitutes were found in 34 percent of saloons.

Saloonkeepers found other ways to turn a profit. Bartenders encouraged treating, which was the custom by which a patron bought a round for everyone in the saloon. Reformers attacked treating, but it was popular with regulars because it promoted male bonding. Some saloons watered spirits or refreshed stale beer with chemicals. Others sold cheap alcohol from bottles that had once contained expensive liquor. Drunkards and children were served. One Ohio seller explained, "We must create the appetite for liquor in the growing boys. Men who drink…will die." Criminal syndicates fenced stolen goods in disreputable drinking houses. At Mickey Finn's Lone Star Saloon in Chicago, customers were invited to try the Mickey Finn Special. After the victim passed out from the drugged drink, he was robbed, beaten, and often stripped. Finn was put out of business in 1903.

A common way to lure customers was the free lunch, which was offered from a buffet table with the purchase of a five-cent glass of beer. To the worker who earned one dollar a day, the free lunch was not a bargain, especially if the salty ham, sardines, potato salad, pickles, and pretzels made him thirsty and led him to buy a second glass of beer, as the seller hoped. A hearty free lunch might draw a large crowd, if the place was close to a factory. Although respectable women did not enter saloons, some working-class bars made an exception. Female factory workers took the free lunch along with a beer in a back room, which they entered through a special side entrance. The idea appalled temperance reformers. The Reverend Mark Matthews of Seattle denounced the saloon: "The most fiendish, corrupt and hell-soaked institution that ever crawled out of the slime of the eternal pit."

Some saloonkeepers gained political power. A voting precinct might be located in the saloon, and the seller became a precinct captain. If voting took place in the back room, chits for free drinks might be given to men who cast ballots, which were not necessarily secret. The proprietor might then advance to elected office. In 1890, eleven of New York City's twenty-four aldermen were saloonkeepers. "It is the degenerate vote that has in the past overwhelmed the liberties of free people," warned Representative Richmond Hobson (D-AL). "And it is the degenerate vote in our big cities that is a menace to our institutions." Muckraking magazines gradually exposed urban corruption practiced by political machines whose power was rooted in saloons. New York's Democratic Party based in Tammany Hall closely resembled the Republican machine that ran Philadelphia. Party bosses were usually Irish Catholic immigrants and their sons or grandsons, and most had ties to saloons. City thievery, payoffs, and prostitution were commonplace. "If we wish to purify politics," said the Anti-Saloon League, "the saloon must be destroyed."

Carry Nation heard the call. Even legally dry Kansas was far from dry. This troubled woman with a stormy family history lived in Kiowa, Kansas, in 1900. Furious at the brazenness of the town's liquor dealers, she took matters into her own hands, literally, and destroyed the fixtures and bottles in the interior of a saloon with a hatchet in the first of her many "smashings." Local officials declined to arrest her. Nation's attack drew national attention, and in 1901 she set off for Topeka, where she used hatchets to smash saloons. When arrested, she resorted to prayer and fasting. Usually an admirer quietly posted bail. Her Topeka campaign drew more publicity, and she took her hatchetations to the East, where the wet press ridiculed her. She continued to attack saloons, but she was careful never to smash a legally licensed place. Nation also organized sell-out performances on Broadway, where she re-created her saloon destructions for the thrill of the curious. A celebrity, Nation continued as an eccentric dry crusader until her death in 1911. Serious dry reformers were embarrassed by her theatrics.

The most powerful and effective anti-liquor organization in the history of the United States was the Anti-Saloon League (ASL), which was founded by evangelical ministers and lawyers in Berea, Ohio, in 1893. The ASL had strong ties to Methodists, Baptists, and Presbyterians. Although many Americans opposed public drunkenness and conceded that alcohol impoverished families and led to terrible crimes, including wife abuse, these same people often found a ban on alcohol to be extreme. Weddings and holiday parties were frequently celebrated with liquor, and many people saw no harm in a glass of wine or beer at home with dinner. Chronic drunkenness in a seedy saloon was different, and immigrant-owned drinking houses lacked respectability. The ASL played on these mixed feelings by stressing opposition to the saloon as an institution. Although the ASL's ultimate goal was national prohibition, the organization placed the saloon front and center with the slogan "The saloon must go!"

5. After the anti-liquor fanatic Carry Nation smashed a saloon in Enterprise, Kansas in 1901, the city marshal led her away to jail.

After testing strategy in the key state of Ohio, the ASL in 1895 became a national organization dedicated to banning alcohol throughout the United States with an amendment to the US Constitution. The ASL attracted both men and women, including many members of the WCTU, although its leadership remained male. The organization had a paid professional staff. In 1903, the national ASL employed 300 staff members; in 1915, 1,500. After Willard's death, the ASL frequently coordinated strategy with the WCTU. Often described as the first political pressure group, the ASL intensely lobbied elected officials, especially state legislators and members of Congress, to pass dry legislation. Unlike the WCTU, the ASL was willing to work with elected officials who drank, so long as officials voted the way the ASL dictated. The approach was based on hard-boiled politics rather than moral fervor.

The ASL believed that there was a dry majority in the United States. "It is the plain church-going people of the towns and the countryside," wrote the progressive reformer Robert Woods, "who by their inherent moral force are bringing about this stupendous achievement." In 1910, half of all Americans lived on farms or in towns with fewer than two thousand people. Pioneering the idea of the single-issue group, the ASL cared only about prohibition. The short-term goal was to dry out as much of the country as possible. The ASL pushed state prohibition where it was viable. If drys could not win statewide, the ASL got states to pass laws allowing local option. After a large number of counties had been made dry and thereby weakened the liquor interests, the ASL sought statewide prohibition. In 1900, thirty-seven states had local option statutes. Meanwhile, alcohol sales were restricted by state laws or local ordinances stopping sales on Sundays, imposing closing hours, limiting the number of liquor licenses, creating dry zones around churches and schools, setting age restrictions, or banning sales to known alcoholics. Once a state was legally dry, the ASL tried to ban the import of alcohol into the state and restrict medicinal use of alcohol.

The methodical and gradual approach of the ASL proved to be more effective than the WCTU's rigid moralism or the Prohibition Party's fanaticism. Gradualism allowed local people to attack key local issues. It also encouraged further political mobilization. "Reforms are not revolutionary," said Ernest Cherrington of the ASL in 1911. "They are evolutionary." Less ideological and more inclusive than the WCTU or Prohibition Party, the ASL also saw increased liquor regulation as the temporary means to reach abolition. Although evangelical Protestant churches were morally opposed to alcohol, they were unable to create an effective political strategy; the ASL provided a political strategy without being committed to a moral absolute, but the organization's strategy harmonized with evangelical goals. The ASL avoided other issues that had distracted the WCTU.

In the one-party South, the ASL supported Democrats, but in the North, the ASL worked with both major parties. In an election in which a wet Republican faced a wet Democrat, the ASL might endorse the Prohibition Party candidate, but it also might sit out the election, since it wanted access to elected officials rather than protest votes. In the case of two dry candidates, the ASL backed the incumbent or the candidate whom the ASL judged best fitted to the jurisdiction for the long run. The ASL provided endorsees with financial aid, temperance press endorsements, church pulpit recommendations, practical assistance in running a campaign, and help with turnout. The organization tried to pass legislation only when it had a majority pre-committed to its agenda. The ASL's presses in Westerville, Ohio, turned out millions of leaflets and pamphlets. In 1907, its *American Issue* had 300,000 monthly subscribers; in 1919, circulation was sixteen million.

After 1900, the Anti-Saloon League benefited from three new political developments. One was the rise of women's suffrage. In western states, where women first gained the vote, the prohibition movement grew as soon as women could vote. "Put the ballot in the hands of woman," preached Charles Locke at the First Methodist Church in Los Angeles, "and she will send the saloons to the damnation of hell." In these states, the ASL tried to keep the liquor issue quiet until women's suffrage passed. In other states, suffragists were urged to hold off until prohibition was won. In reality, women voted about the same way as men, although dry women were energized by having the ballot. In 1917, there were nineteen dry states. In five western states women's suffrage preceded prohibition, but prohibition came first in the other fourteen states.

The second change was the rise of the Progressive movement. Although reformers were split on prohibition, many Progressives endorsed the idea because they saw saloonkeepers as key players in corrupt political machines, liquor sales were often tied to gambling and prostitution, and alcohol played a major role in family destruction. Both drys and Progressives stressed a scientific approach, the use of experts, fact finding, social research, and statistics. Southern Progressives, in particular, embraced prohibition, perhaps because it enabled them to enjoy powerful evangelical support while avoiding economic questions that threatened the power of the southern white elite.

Finally, beginning in 1903, Wayne Wheeler, an Ohio-born lawyer and Congregationalist, proved to be a brilliant political strategist for the ASL at first in Ohio and then in Washington, DC. He threatened elected officials who opposed the ASL with annihilation at the ballot box, and his electoral prowess intimidated many politicians. Large campaign contributions and masses of dry volunteers usually brought electoral success. Local option was used to dry out rural areas. ASL-sponsored local option elections featured children's parades and temperance bands. To stoke enthusiasm, the ASL imported popular speakers, including the former major-league baseball player turned evangelical temperance reformer Billy Sunday. "The saloonkeeper and the devil are both pulling on the same rope," he argued. Wets countered with the attorney Clarence Darrow, who denounced "fanaticism and intolerance." The next step was statewide prohibition. However, great cities like New York, Chicago, and San Francisco kept New York State, Illinois, and California wet. After most states were dry, Wheeler planned to get an amendment to the US Constitution passed to capture the holdouts. "A national evil requires a national remedy," he said in 1917. The plan was to encircle the wet cities and then cut off their liquor.

During the Progressive Era, increased scientific knowledge about alcohol produced disturbing new findings. In 1909, Professor

Winfield Hall of Northwestern University stated, "Alcohol is a narcotic in its drug action." Alcohol was a depressant, caused a decline in mental capacity, and resulted in loss of muscular control. This information flooded the new middle-class magazines. Life insurers reported that drinkers had shorter lives, and medical researchers linked alcohol abuse to insanity and degenerate children. Scientists constantly reduced the amount of strong drink that could be considered safe, and fewer physicians wrote prescriptions for distilled spirits. Social scientists linked drinking, crime, poverty, and prostitution. The National Conference of Charities calculated that alcohol was responsible for 50 percent of crime, 45 percent of desertion of children, 42 percent of broken homes, and 25 percent of poverty. Leading dry Progressives included Jane Addams of Chicago's Hull House and Robert Woods of Boston's South End Settlement House, as well as the economist Irving Fisher of Yale.

Between 1907 and 1916, dry forces won major victories at the state level, particularly in the South and West. Oklahoma was admitted to the Union in 1907 with a dry constitution that established statewide prohibition. Southern states suddenly shifted into the dry column. In the aftermath of the Atlanta race riot of 1906, the Georgia legislature passed statewide prohibition in 1907. Women paraded and lobbied legislators prior to the vote. The main argument was to protect southern white women from rapes by drunken black men. Racial hysteria appeared frequently in southern dry campaigns. The anti-liquor cause was aided by the rise of cheap liquor distilled in St. Louis for the southern African American market. Many brands had vulgar names. One, called Black Cock Vigor Gin, had a label that featured a partially nude white woman. Alabama, North Carolina, and Mississippi adopted statewide prohibition in 1908, and Tennessee joined the list in 1909. By January 1917, there were ten dry southern states. Some African Americans who were denied access to liquor switched to cocaine, which was legal.

During these same years, a number of western states also adopted statewide prohibition. In 1914, Washington, Oregon, Colorado, and Arizona went dry at the ballot box. In all four states the voters acted after the legislature had declined to do so. By late 1917, there were twenty-three dry states, seventeen of which had gone dry by popular vote. How well did these laws function? "Kansas has prohibition, and among the rural population it is fairly well enforced," noted the *Los Angeles Times* in a 1915 editorial. "But in the cities there is a supply of blind pigs whose styes [*sic*] are crowded with worshipers of Bacchus." Not only was there an urban-rural split, but prohibition also played differently across class lines. The policy threatened the working-class saloon, while the middle class used the mail to import alcohol for personal consumption. The *Boston Transcript*, the voice of the New England elite, was blunt: "So long as the well-to-do individual was free to import liquors for his own use he has often inclined to favor prohibition enactments for the 'lower classes.' " Ethnicity and class were often identical. In Boston, the lower classes were Irish immigrants.

The remaining wet states included major markets such as New York, Illinois, and California, each of which was home to a hard-drinking city. Trying to dry out such places was a gargantuan task. New York City alone had thirteen thousand saloons, and the state's per capita consumption of alcohol was three and a half times the national average. Many wets, however, were complacent. In 1916, the Congress of Hotel Associations met in New York. One hotelier told the *New York Times*, "The great American hotel will never go dry because the great majority don't want that kind of a hotel." Nevertheless, the rural-dominated New York State legislature authorized local option in 1917.

America's great cities were teeming with immigrants. In 1910, 14.9 percent of Americans were foreign-born; they were concentrated in the fast-growing, populous, industrial cities. In New York and

Chicago, immigrants and their children were a majority of the population. Most came from hard-drinking European cultures. Many immigrants lived and worked in ethnic enclaves; their saloons were sanctuaries. As prohibition gained strength, so did the wet urban backlash. On November 7, 1915, forty-four thousand wets paraded in Chicago carrying banners in many languages. A coffin in a buggy was labeled "Here lies our liberty." On the same day, Representative Richmond Hobson, the Alabama prohibitionist, spoke at Chicago's Second Presbyterian Church, which was along the wet parade route. As the noisy protesters passed the church, he blasted the "parade of degenerates."

One could feel the pressure building inside President Woodrow Wilson's new administration in 1913. In 1911, Wilson had appeared to favor statewide prohibition in Texas by citing the state's "homogeneity," but in 1912, in need of support for the presidential nomination from both dry southerners and wet big-city machines, he endorsed local option. Leaning in the popular direction, Wilson declined to serve wine in the White House, and Secretary of State William Jennings Bryan, an evangelical, a teetotaler, and a prohibitionist, substituted grape juice at receptions. Diplomats responded with mirth and scorn. Bryan considered demanding a teetotal pledge from all State Department employees. Secretary of the Navy Josephus Daniels, another dry, banned alcohol from the US Navy.

As dry territory expanded, so did alcohol consumption. The best explanation for this paradox was increasing importation of alcohol across state lines for personal use. The brewers and distillers who shipped it thrived. "The success of the mail order business," noted an official of the National Model License League in 1910, "has been proportionate to the spread of 'dry' territory." In the first half of December 1911, forty-five railroad cars filled with Christmas cheer arrived in dry Macon, Georgia. Producers solicited sales in many newspapers and magazines, which angered the dry forces. Alabama made it a crime to sell an out-of-state newspaper that contained liquor advertising, so a Birmingham news dealer carefully cut out the ads before he sold the papers.

In 1913, Wayne Wheeler of the Anti-Saloon League decided to cut off this out-of-state supply. Riding the reform wave and threatening to unseat uncooperative incumbents, Wheeler persuaded Congress to pass the Webb-Kenyon Act, which made it illegal to ship alcohol into a state that banned it, even if the product was for personal use. Prohibition advocates began to distinguish between dry states, where retail sales were illegal, and bone-dry states, where importation even for personal use was barred. At the time, only three states were bone-dry. Because of the interstate commerce clause in the US Constitution, many observers thought that the Supreme Court would overturn Webb-Kenyon. Wheeler personally argued the dry case before the justices, and in January 1917 the high court cited congressional power to control interstate commerce to validate the law by a vote of 7–2. In this era, the court was inclined to accept Progressive legislation. Similarly, the court upheld the Harrison Narcotics Tax Act (1914), which brought opiates under federal control for the first time.

After 1865, the federal government's income had come primarily from customs duties on imports and taxes on alcohol. In the 1880s, alcohol taxes had provided as much as 40 percent of federal revenue; in 1914, 35 percent. Collection of the tax was not always easy, particularly in southern Appalachia. In 1892, Democrats won both the presidency and Congress. Ideologically committed to lower tariff duties, Democrats decided in 1894 to finance the government by reestablishing the Civil War–era income tax. Wealthy northern urban Republicans were targeted for this tax. Lower tariffs would reduce the price of imported goods and put pressure on the price of all manufactures, which would benefit rural southerners and westerners who had voted Democratic.

In 1895, the US Supreme Court, in a 5–4 vote, overturned the income tax because it violated a provision in the US Constitution

6. Large piles of wooden kegs and shipping containers at this Topeka freight station in the early 1900s tangibly indicated that local drinkers legally imported large quantities of alcohol.

that said taxes had to be levied proportionate to state population. Some observers suspected that the real reason the justices ruled as they did was that they were wet. Had the income tax remained in place, prohibition forces would have tried to substitute the income tax for alcohol taxes in order to ban alcohol. In 1909, Congress sent the Sixteenth Amendment, which allowed a federal income tax, to the states, and after it was ratified in 1913, the Wilson administration and the Democratic Congress enacted a small income tax on a very few wealthy taxpayers. Drys could now seek a constitutional amendment to ban alcohol without worrying about the loss of liquor revenue, since the income tax could be increased to make up the difference.

In 1914, the Anti-Saloon League demanded that Congress vote on a constitutional amendment banning alcohol, even though the amendment could not win two-thirds in either the House or the Senate. Representative Richmond Hobson (D-AL) introduced the measure in the House. A Spanish-American War admiral, Hobson told drys on the Capitol steps, "The principles of war are the same whether it is a war between nations or a war between civilians and its destroying foe, the liquor traffic." Although senators who did not want to be put on the spot blocked a vote in the Senate, Wayne Wheeler held sufficient influence to insist that the House take a vote. On December 22, 1914, the drys won a majority, 197–189, but not the necessary two-thirds. Progressive Party members voted yes, 15–1. The ASL then moved to defeat members who had cast "no" votes in the 1916 election. After wets were routed at the polls, the ASL realized that the new Congress meeting after March 1917 could pass a dry amendment.

In the years from 1900 to 1916, the alcohol industry fought back hard against the growing demands for prohibition coming from the WCTU, the ASL, and dry Progressive reformers. Producers tried to elect wet candidates and financed the wet side in local option or statewide votes on prohibition. The distillers, however, had been discredited in the whiskey tax scandal in the 1870s, and few elected officials wanted ties to that industry. Winemakers had no political influence outside California, the only state with substantial wine production and consumption. So the defense of alcohol fell to the brewers, who had the most to lose, since they controlled most saloons. Between 1880 and 1900, the number of saloons doubled to 300,000 and the per capita consumption of beer also doubled. After 1900, beer consumption continued to grow. Declining to defend distilled liquor, brewers promoted beer as a moderate, low-alcohol, healthful drink. "We deem it particularly deplorable that a few brewers are attempting to obtain legislative advantages for beer at the expense of other alcoholic beverages," the New York State Wholesale Liquor Dealers' Association complained in the *New York Times* in 1916. Distillers refused to assist the brewers in the campaign to stop prohibition. Later, both brewers and distillers realized that their infighting had sabotaged the alcohol industry.

Only in the wettest areas inhabited by immigrants from Ireland, Germany, Italy, or Eastern Europe did any office seeker openly take campaign contributions from brewers or saloonkeepers. The brewers devised a subterfuge. Kaiser Wilhelm II had established the German-American Alliance in 1900 to promote friendship between the people of the United States and those of the German Empire. It had two million members in 1914, when one-quarter of Americans had German ancestry. The German government financed the Alliance, which promoted German culture and gave immigrants ties to their native land. Cynics suspected darker purposes. In the event of a European war, the Alliance would rally German Americans to the German side, help keep America neutral, and, if war broke out between the United States and Germany, organize espionage and sabotage inside the United States. In 1915, 550 delegates representing 10,000 local affiliates in forty-five states met at the Alliance's biennial convention in San Francisco. This famously wet organization adopted a report opposing national prohibition.

The brewers supported wet candidates or wet positions in referenda by funneling money through the German-American Alliance. The Alliance lobbyist in Washington, DC, was Julius Moersch, who was also the lobbyist for the National Liquor Dealers Association. The Alliance then transferred money to wet office seekers or to campaign committees organized to defeat local option or statewide prohibition referenda. Its funds paid for leaflets, rallies, speakers, hall rent, and decorations, as well as hiring beaters to get out the vote on Election Day. Much of the money was spent on newspaper advertising or inserting wet stories into rural or small-town newspapers. Brewers also financed the wet journalist Arthur Brisbane's purchase of the *Washington Times*. The usual argument was that prohibition was an extreme response to alcohol abuse. Wets advocated responsible use of a light beverage consumed in moderation and saw each American as a free person who had a right to decide whether or not to drink. Personal liberty had been very effective in destroying prohibition during the 1850s, and it remained the single most potent wet argument until prohibition ended in 1933.

The United States Brewers' Association (USBA), the trade group whose meeting minutes were kept in German, controlled the wet campaign. As prohibition became a more serious threat, the USBA, led by the charismatic brewer Adolphus Busch, assessed each member 3 cents a barrel. The Alliance sent this money to the states, counties, and cities where it was needed. Busch was a brilliant businessman with an ambiguous national identity. The family owned a lot of property in Germany, including one large castle, and the company imported the hops it used in St. Louis from Central Europe. After Adolphus Busch died in 1913, his widow, a German immigrant to the United States who had never acquired US citizenship, spent time in Germany. She happened to be at the castle when the war started, and she used her citizenship to save the family's German property during World War I. Meanwhile, their American-born son, August Busch, who could not be a dual citizen under American law, used his American citizenship to save the family's property in the United States.

In 1911, there had been an ugly statewide prohibition battle in the key state of Texas, where beer had been a local staple since German immigrants arrived before the Civil War. When wets narrowly won the statewide vote, the dry forces charged "wholesale fraud." There was widespread vote-buying in Mexican American areas, and wet urban machines allowed double voting; they made sure drunks voted by carrying them to the polls. On the other side, the *New York Times* reported that dry supporters had visited African American homes in the middle of the night before the election to warn against voting. What most enraged the drys, however, was the tremendous money that backed the wet side, which made powerful and effective use of leaflets, pamphlets, newspaper ads, planted articles, and cash. Drys had only women, who did not yet have the vote in Texas; evangelical preachers; and a handful of prominent politicians, including Morris Sheppard, who went on to the US Senate and would sponsor the Eighteenth Amendment.

Texas saloons and brewers denied that they had spent money on the referendum. To do so would have violated Texas election laws, which the dry legislature had engineered to prevent liquor money from buying a victory. The drys forced another statewide referendum in 1914, when Texas voters again narrowly rejected prohibition. This time the Texas attorney general filed an anti-trust lawsuit against several state brewers who owned or controlled many tied-house saloons. When the brewery and saloon records were subpoenaed, they revealed that the industry had been telling a partial truth about wet expenditures in the two elections. In 1915, the public learned that in the 1911 referendum, the St. Louis brewer Adolphus Busch had written a letter offering a personal $100,000 campaign contribution.

World War I began in Europe in 1914, and although the United States did not enter the war until 1917, tension rose between the United States and Germany from the beginning. Not only did Americans sympathize with Britain and France as democracies, but American trade was tied to London. As the British and French sold foreign assets to buy food and military supplies in the United States, Americans worried that the Germans would engage in sabotage against American industry that aided the Allied side. In 1915, the National Civic Federation, a private investigative service, discovered a plot in a German saloon in Paterson, New Jersey, to blow up munitions plants. German saboteurs destroyed dozens of ships and burned many American munitions plants. The insurance industry was alarmed. Just how and where did the German government recruit its saboteurs? Many Americans suspected saloons and beer gardens where German Americans gathered.

In 1916, the public learned that wet money spent in the Texas prohibition referenda in 1911 and 1914 as well as in other states had come from the kaiser-funded German-American Alliance. As it turned out, the kaiser had not provided any contributions. Instead, the funds had come from the American brewing industry, especially from the Busch family. The brewers had deceived the public by hiding their role in funding the wet campaign, and they had used as their vehicle the official German government-sponsored Alliance. They had tried to hide the tie between the brewers and the Alliance, and they had also hidden the tie between the Alliance and the expenditures. The German-American Alliance's wetness was not just about an immigrant community's love of beer. The Texas brewers were charged with violating the state's election laws. Seven local brewers and two out-of-state brewers, including Busch, pled nolo contendere and paid a $289,000 fine.

In spring 1916, the *New York World* published documents showing that the German-American Alliance had supported the German war effort since 1914. The *New York Times* called the revelations "astounding." Given dry charges that the German government was trying to weaken the United States militarily, economically, and morally, the result was devastating. By late 1916, no American office seeker could take campaign funds from either the brewers or the German American community. Suddenly, even before the United States entered the war against Germany in April 1917, the wets were disarmed. In November, Wayne Wheeler warned, "The liquor traffic...is the strong financial supporter of the German-American Alliance. The purpose of this alliance is to secure German solidarity...and oppose any restriction or prohibition of the liquor traffic." The next year, Congress revoked the charter of the German-American Alliance, which vanished overnight. By then, orchestras had stopped playing German music and sauerkraut had become "liberty cabbage." George Sutherland, a dry leader in Minnesota, said, "The question for every American citizen to decide now is whether he is for this country or for the Kaiser."

The world war also aided the American dry cause. Early in the war, the Russian government abolished its state distillery system in favor of wartime prohibition. Widely praised at the time, this disastrous policy deprived the government of needed revenue, led to massive illicit distilling, and helped bring down the tsar's regime. Britain restricted the amount of grain available for brewing and distilling, imposed a liquor ban in a few key industrial areas, shortened the hours that alcohol could be sold, and adopted state-run public houses in the industrial district in Carlisle, England. Canada, which had entered the war in 1914 and was a major food supplier to Britain, adopted wartime prohibition. Alcohol restrictions had global appeal. After the war, prohibition continued for a few years in most Canadian provinces, Finland banned beverages having more than 2 percent alcohol until 1932, and Norway stopped the sale of distilled spirits until 1927.

Events in the United States moved quickly in 1917. The new Congress, which normally would not have met until December 1917, was called into special session on April 2 after German submarines had attacked American shipping in the Atlantic. Four days later, Congress declared war against Germany. France and especially Britain were running short of food, much of which had to be imported. The progressive magazine the *Independent* asked, "Shall the many have food, or the few have drink?" To save food, Congress in August passed the Lever Food and Fuel Control Act, which provided that no foodstuffs could be distilled. The brewers' union played a role in getting beer exempted. Hard liquor that was in storage could be sold, but new whiskey could not be made. To conserve foodstuffs further, in December President Woodrow Wilson issued an executive order, as permitted by the statute, to cut the amount of grain that could be brewed by 30 percent, and he ordered that all beer be only 2.75 percent alcohol, which was one-third to one-half below normal strength. In July 1918, Wilson cut brewers' coal allotments by 50 percent.

The Selective Service Act passed in May 1917 called American men for military service. The new law banned alcohol from training camps and adjacent areas. Not every jurisdiction complied, including a defiantly wet St. Paul, Minnesota, which was close to Fort Snelling. The US Army inspector general told the press, "Conditions [are] worse here than anywhere I know of.... [I]f I had my way I would withdraw the soldiers, [and] lock the doors on the Snelling barracks." The military restriction greatly expanded the number of places in the country that were dry. Congress also banned soldiers from being served alcohol in uniform. Of course, when the doughboys got to France they found plenty of wine, although it seldom reached the trenches. The military introduced cigarettes to the troops as a substitute for alcohol. Nicotine kept soldiers awake on guard duty, which alcohol did not do. Hundreds of thousands of soldiers became addicted to cigarettes.

On December 18, 1917, Congress passed the Eighteenth Amendment and sent it to the states for ratification. The House vote was 282–128; Senate, 47–8. Although the prohibition amendment was closely identified with Senator Morris Sheppard (D-TX), its main sponsor in the Senate, it was largely written by Wayne Wheeler, who had constructed the measure to get the two-thirds vote in each house. It is worth quoting the first and second paragraphs in full:

> Section 1. After one year from the ratification of this article the manufacture, sale, or transportation of intoxicating liquors within, the importation thereof into, or the exportation thereof from the United States and all territory subject to the jurisdiction thereof for beverage purposes is hereby prohibited.

Section 2. The Congress and the several states shall have concurrent power to enforce this article by appropriate legislation.

A third section provided that the states had seven years from the date of submission to ratify the amendment. Ratification was completed on January 16, 1919.

Brewers and distillers demanded compensation for their property. As a matter of principle, drys were unwilling to pay one cent to the alcohol industry. The one-year delay from ratification to implementation was designed to give the industry time to sell off its stock and enter other businesses. As the press noted at the time, the amendment did not ban drinking, nor did it ban storing pre-prohibition alcohol in one's home for later use. Neither *possession* nor *purchase* was illegal, although *selling* was. Buying was not banned because prosecutors wanted to use buyers to testify against sellers. Under the home possession provision, the wealthy banker J. P. Morgan laid in one thousand cases of French champagne and prepared to outlast prohibition. The Yale Club in New York City also stored alcohol and did not run out of its pre-prohibition supply until the month that prohibition was repealed. In reality, only the wealthy could take advantage of this storage provision.

The amendment did not define intoxicating liquors. By using this phrase, Wheeler hinted to brewers, vintners, and their customers that hard liquor was the target. A few wets naively believed that the amendment banned only distilled spirits. What percentage of alcohol made a drink intoxicating? In 1917 no general agreement existed on this issue, but the amendment's second clause gave Congress the power to legislate the answer. Even "intoxicating liquors" might be produced if they were not for "beverage purposes." Both industrial and medicinal alcohol were acceptable. Many old-fashioned physicians and pharmacists prescribed whiskey, which had been used in dry cities, counties, or states for decades. Again, Congress (or the states) would set the limits. Moreover,

Catholics, Episcopalians, Jews, and a few other practitioners used wine in religious ceremonies. As a practical matter, Wheeler knew that sacramental wine could not be banned. Congress would have to provide detailed rules about that matter, too.

Finally, the amendment's second section created a confusing dual federal and state jurisdiction over alcohol. Drys included this provision because they were nervous about the future. Without joint control, a future wet Congress might repeal dry federal enforcement, and without dual jurisdiction, dry states might be left with no enforcement power. Drys were even more worried about wet states that might decline to provide state enforcement. Concurrent jurisdiction allowed the federal government to enforce the amendment if the state refused to do so. This became a real issue in the 1920s. Nowhere else does the Constitution provide dual federal and state enforcement of a constitutional provision. During the 1920s, dual jurisdiction caused constant trouble, and the Twenty First Amendment repealing prohibition would ultimately give the states control of alcohol policy.

Drys were confident that the amendment would be ratified by the necessary thirty-six of the forty-eight states within seven years. Most temperance leaders expected ratification within several years. At the moment the amendment passed Congress, twenty-seven states were dry. To the surprise of everyone, the amendment proved to be wildly popular. Ratification took little more than one year. In forty-six legislatures that voted approval, 80 percent of legislators voted yes. Only Connecticut and Rhode Island rejected the amendment. There were several reasons for this rapid approval. The amendment was caught up in Progressive Era enthusiasm for reform. Dry reformers had talked about a national constitutional amendment for decades, so the idea was not new. Then, too, legislatures had rural majorities. "Urbanization," wrote the dry Elizabeth Tilton in her diary, "had not yet laid its material, beer-soaked class on the vote in America." Drys also exploited the concept of wartime sacrifice. If young Americans could be sent to die in the war in France, then those who were fortunate enough to be at home should at least sacrifice the comfort of alcohol. Moral fervor ran high. The publisher William Randolph Hearst wrote, "The suppression of the drink traffic is an expression of the higher morality upon which we are now embarking."

Distillers and brewers were paralyzed. Both industries were associated with irresponsible public behavior, that is, drunkenness, and neither fitted the wartime call for hard work. In addition, the brewers were suspected of sympathy for Germany. The ASL denounced "the un-American, pro-German… treasonable liquor traffic." Wartime patriotism stressed conformity, and it was hard to call lager beer American. The war challenged the old order, and the saloon became an embarrassment. Given the large margins by which legislatures voted for ratification during 1918 and early 1919, it is clear that the amendment, at least temporarily, enjoyed robust support. There are no polls for 1918, but during World War II, Gallup found a rising support for prohibition that subsided when the war ended. Without World War I, it is doubtful that prohibition would ever have passed Congress or been ratified.

Faced with food shortages, President Wilson used his wartime powers to ban brewing after December 1, 1918. Although the war ended on November 11, Congress passed wartime prohibition a week later. This law banned production of beer or wine after May 1, 1919, and the sale of alcohol after July 1, 1919, except for half-a-percent near-beer. Both provisions were to remain in effect until the troops were demobilized. On June 30, 1919, St. Paul had a rowdy drinking celebration on the last evening before wartime prohibition took effect. In many saloons, patrons threw out the clocks. The law went into effect in 1919 because the war had ended with an armistice rather than German surrender; a peace treaty was needed to end the war. When the Treaty of Versailles failed in the Senate in 1919, the United States and Germany technically remained at war. As a result, wartime prohibition continued until the Eighteenth Amendment went into effect in January 1920.

The new Republican Congress elected in 1918 contained even more drys than the previous Democratic Congress. To ensure that prohibition did not become a partisan issue, Wayne Wheeler always wanted dry majorities in both parties. The change in party control shifted leadership on the liquor issue from Senator Morris Sheppard to Representative Andrew Volstead (R-MN). In September 1919, Volstead, along with the ASL, drafted the Volstead Act, which defined the terms and provided the details left out of the Eighteenth Amendment. Wilson vetoed the bill, but Congress passed the bill over his veto in October. The measure superseded wartime prohibition when the Eighteenth Amendment went into effect in January 1920. To the disappointment of many moderates, Volstead rejected Wilson's early wartime 2.75 percent beer. Instead, the legal limit for intoxicating liquor was set at 0.5 percent. This particular limit was picked because it was the lowest amount of alcohol that could be detected; it had nothing to do with intoxication. Today, such products are sold as non-alcoholic beer.

The Volstead Act did allow farmers to make hard apple cider for their own consumption, but the beverage could neither be sold nor transported. Home-brewed beer was banned, but the federal government issued permits allowing wine to be made for family use. All sorts of mischief came from that provision. Rabbis, priests, and other clergy who needed sacramental wine were authorized to obtain wine from specially licensed sources. The Beaulieu winery in California supplied the Roman Catholic Church throughout the United States, and the winery became the largest vintner in the country, a position it continued to hold for years after the repeal of prohibition. Subject to state law, physicians could write limited prescriptions for medicinal whiskey, which pharmacists had to fill using federal order pads.

7. During World War I, dry forces used patriotic, especially anti-German, arguments to push wartime prohibition.

The Volstead Act gave enforcement to the new Prohibition Bureau. From the beginning, the agency was incompetent and corrupt. Wayne Wheeler, who controlled all appointments, ignored law enforcement qualifications in favor of political patronage and church connections. The bureau was under Internal Revenue inside the Treasury Department. Later, the Prohibition Bureau was a separate Treasury unit, and it was subsequently transferred to the Justice Department. J. Edgar Hoover rejected proposals that prohibition be enforced by the Bureau of Investigation (i.e., the FBI); he saw no advantage in getting involved in the issue. The Coast Guard got the unenviable job of interdicting liquor illegally entering or leaving the United States by water. Enforcement turned out to be far more challenging than the dry forces ever imagined.

The dry crusade

Chapter 3
Prohibition

January 16, 1920, was the last day that Americans could legally buy a drink before both the Eighteenth Amendment and the Volstead Act went into effect. At the stroke of midnight, the country was set to go dry. In the great cities, revelers treated the evening like New Year's Eve. Saloons, cafes, cabarets, dance halls, hotel bars, and gourmet restaurants hung festive decorations, served special food, and played music, while patrons ate, drank, and danced. All evening, celebrants downed glass after glass of their favorite and soon to be forbidden alcoholic beverages. No city turned out in greater force than did New York, which was often considered the wettest city on the continent. As midnight approached, the band played, and patrons raised their glasses ironically to toast the beginning of dry America. When the clock struck twelve, drinkers downed their last drop of legal liquor accompanied by cheers, jeers, whistles, and noisemakers. Then celebrants looked at their empty glasses and called for another glass. In most places, waiters obliged. How long did prohibition last in New York? About two minutes, or however long it took to obtain a new glass.

Whenever a substance is banned, two things happen. First, the price goes up, and second, the product returns in a more concentrated form, or a replacement appears. The high risk of handling an item that has low value leads to potent substitutes that can be readily made, shipped, and stored. Thus, the ban on opium under the Harrison Act (1914) yielded heroin, the war against cocaine in the 1970s produced crack, and the prohibition of alcohol caused a shift from beer to hard liquor, and the substitution of opiates. In many parts of the country, the illegal production of beer was problematic. The beverage spoiled quickly, it was too bulky to hide, and hijacking of delivery trucks was common. Distilled spirits were cheaper to produce, storage was easier, and the higher price per gallon for spirits helped compensate for the risk of handling an illegal substance. Beer existed during prohibition, especially in New York, Chicago, and a few other great cities, but the standard drink was distilled spirits. Prohibition brought back the very hard liquor that the original temperance movement had despised.

In the early 1920s, supplying liquor was largely a mom-and-pop operation. Saloons and restaurants tried to stay open and serve customers alcoholic substitutes for their regular drinks. Bootleggers supplied imports immediately. In 1920, a pilot landed a cargo of eighteen cases of Canadian liquor at an airstrip near Des Moines, Iowa. Asking $250 per twelve-bottle case, more than six times the pre-prohibition price, he sold out in two hours and flew away before the police even knew he had arrived. This type of high-quality imported liquor was likely to be cut with low-quality local spirits, which moonshiners instantly supplied. Distillation was simple, and kitchen stills and bathtub gin became a reality. This new moonshine, unlike commercial American whiskey, was not aged. White lightning was colorless and biting, and it usually had to be drunk with a flavorful mixer to mask the foul taste. Soft drinks and fruit juices were favored.

In North Georgia and other parts of Appalachia, farmers who had always done a certain amount of home distillation of corn liquor for family and friends were happy to expand production to meet market demand. Hardware stores sold portable stills. Retail prices for moonshine shot up three to five times. High prices provided the incentive to scale up production, even when distillers balanced the chances of being caught by federal agents. A short prison term might be a bargain if they could make enough money selling illegal moonshine before they were arrested. After World War I, the value of the dollar, compared with other global currencies, had risen so high that the United States lost its grain export markets. The twenties brought low farm prices and rising farm foreclosures, so wherever grain was grown, some farmers liquefied their crops to make moonshine. Poor white women and African Americans were also involved in small-scale rural distillation. In addition, blacks commonly tended white-owned stills, which made them vulnerable to arrest.

In the Midwest, some farmers also defied dry expectations. Irish and German Catholic immigrants had settled Carroll County, Iowa, in the mid-1800s, and they had never accepted local, state, or national prohibition. The county priest assured locals that illegal liquor was no sin; indeed, the priest allowed moonshine to be distilled in the church basement. When federal prohibition arrived, Joe Irlbeck was a twenty-year-old farm laborer who was shocked to find that spirits cost $10 a gallon. He needed a quart to drink for the weekend, and that would cost nearly half a week's pay. So he decided to distill his own liquor. In the twenties the county's struggling farmers formed a co-op to sell corn and rye to Irlbeck, who eventually ran one of the biggest moonshine operations in the United States. The county produced a high-quality product, Templeton Rye, which was sold locally, but to gain wider distribution, the distiller had to deal with mobsters, including the Al Capone gang in Chicago. Templeton Rye commanded the highest price of any domestic product in Chicago's speakeasies. Although the liquor contained some rye, it was mostly sugar, which distilled more quickly.

A wet consensus, a wet sheriff, and payoffs protected moonshine in Carroll County, but danger came from the federal Prohibition Bureau's Benjamin F. Wilson, who knew the area. The honest, diligent, and resourceful Wilson was an exceptional agent. Most political appointees like him had a bad reputation. Brooklyn US attorney William Ross called them "absolutely crooked." *Variety* observed in 1922, "The federal men…are doing more to make prohibition detested than anyone else, even the drys." That year, Wilson raided Carroll County. Using thirty-eight search warrants, he seized 2,500 gallons of mash and 125 gallons of spirits. Sixteen moonshiners eventually pled guilty and paid small fines. Local juries would not convict violators, so Wilson brought the cases in federal court in Fort Dodge. Wilson staged only sporadic raids in the county because he had to operate elsewhere in Iowa. Carroll County residents were not afraid of Wilson's infrequent visits. They made a lot of liquor and money during his absence.

Carroll County residents were more afraid of the Ku Klux Klan, which had been organized in neighboring dry evangelical Protestant counties. Concerned about the government's lax enforcement of prohibition, the Klan invaded Carroll County to impose its own peculiar form of law and order. One Ku Kluxer explained that an excellent way to obtain liquor was to seize it while marauding with the Klan. In many parts of the United States, the Klan attacked distilleries or wet shipments. "If local officials cannot enforce the law," vowed one Klan leader and Methodist minister in Denver, Colorado, "we should teach them how." The Indiana Klan's magazine, the *Fiery Cross*, promised, "The Klan is going to drive bootlegging out of this land." In Williamson County, Illinois, the federal Prohibition Bureau agent in charge deputized hundreds of Klansmen from neighboring counties to assist in a series of simultaneous raids. The resulting deadly mayhem led higher-ups in the Prohibition Bureau to replace the head agent.

In most rural areas, farmer-distillers had to be wary. Neighbors might call the authorities, or producers might turn in their rivals to reduce competition and gain a local monopoly. To be allowed to distill for commercial sale required campaign contributions, payoffs, or bribes to elected officials, who often allowed the moonshining to continue but insisted on a large share of the profits. Local markets were necessarily small because the population was small, many people were abstainers, and others lacked cash. To make significant money, the farmer-distiller had to join a larger distribution network. The stills were in the country, but the thirst was in the cities. Distillers in Carroll County, Iowa, looked to Des Moines and Chicago. Making contacts with buyers could be risky, producers could be cheated out of payments, or urban gangs might come to steal liquor from a known still or even demand the sale of the entire property at a very low price.

Getting the goods to market posed a challenge. State and federal authorities, acting on tips, set up roadblocks. Hijackings were a greater problem. Rivals stole the loads, or sometimes the thief was the pre-arranged buyer, so payment would not have to be made for a shipment. Thugs or prohibition agents sometimes stole cars or trucks, and sometimes drivers got shot. There were dangerous high-speed chases on unpaved roads. Few distillers drove their own loads because if they were caught, authorities would search the farm, destroy the still and any alcohol, and seize the property. Any property used in the production, distribution, or sale of alcohol was subject to forfeiture. A distiller risked grain, firewood, the still, liquor inventory, and the farm; a driver could lose only an automobile. In 1924, the Prohibition Bureau seized 5,214 such automobiles. To escape police and hijackers, drivers used Whiskey Sixes: six-cylinder Buicks or Studebakers with souped-up engines, heavy springs, and extra storage compartments. Southern drivers tested their cars in races against each other, which later became the basis for the NASCAR racing industry.

Rural moonshiners could not, however, slake the thirst of the cities. One possibility was to act within the Volstead Act to produce beer that had less than half a percent alcohol. In 1918, Anheuser-Busch spent $10 million to build a giant near-beer brewery in St. Louis. Heavily advertised, Bevo sold well for a few months in 1920, but sales quickly dropped after drinkers found that Bevo lacked a kick. Production dwindled, although Iowans liked to spike near beer with hard liquor, including Templeton Rye.

The best way to make non-alcoholic beer was to brew regular beer and then remove the alcohol. This process led to the diversion of the original alcoholic beer to speakeasies. In 1922, 200 of 500 licensed brewers were cited for violations. "The working classes demand their beer," declared Governor Emanuel Philipp (R-WI) in 1920. In the mid-1920s brewers sold non-alcoholic malt syrup and malt extract. When customers added water and yeast, the substance turned into beer or malt for distillation. Robust sales continued until the end of prohibition. "If you really want to know," Gussie Busch later said, "we ended up as the biggest bootlegging supply house in the United States."

Urban distillation was one possibility, but it had limitations. Only the smallest kitchen stills could be hidden in a city. Even then, neighbors who learned about the activity might demand free liquor, which cut into profits. Producers also used small kitchen alcohol cookers to remove poisons from industrial alcohol. Italian women frequently ran these businesses, and they sometimes made wine as well as liquor. Criminal gangs quickly gained control. In Brooklyn, the mobster Frankie Yale paid Italian families $15 a day to maintain stills in their homes. In Pittsburgh, working-class women who produced or sold small amounts of alcohol were the most likely wets to be arrested. The police searched homes without warrants, looking both for alcohol and for signs of union organizing. Cities also had large commercial stills, but getting grain or other material without being noticed was a problem. Such distilleries could only be operated with payoffs to police and elected officials. The quality was low, the technology was unsophisticated, and these distilled products were often mixed with other, higher quality liquors.

Another source of liquor throughout the twenties was industrial alcohol, which was distilled legally by special federal permit in large quantities. Alcohol was used in paint, in antifreeze, and as a solvent in many mechanical processes. Production rose from 28 million gallons in 1920 to 81 million gallons in 1925, when chief prohibition enforcer Lincoln Andrews estimated that 90 percent of all bootleg liquor contained at least some denatured industrial alcohol. To prevent its use in beverages, the government required the industry to add toxic chemicals to this alcohol. As a practical matter, it was cheaper and easier for the industry to distill pure alcohol (which could be drunk) and then add poison. This gave unscrupulous manufacturers the ability to divert some drinkable product for illegal sale as a beverage prior to treatment. While most additives had a foul smell or taste, this was not always true. Some industrial processes required tasteless and odorless poisons. Druggists bought bootleg denatured alcohol for $3.50 to $4.00 per gallon rather than pay $5.00 for legal alcohol, which included $4.18 of tax and considerable red tape.

Bootleggers often cut their own product by adding cheap industrial alcohol. An illegal side industry developed in removing toxins; if they could be purged, then industrial alcohol might yield a big profit. Unfortunately, the amateur chemists sometimes produced deadly results. As injuries and deaths grew, so did the public outcry, but both the government and dry forces wanted to punish drinkers of industrial alcohol. After several New Yorkers died and hundreds were sickened by bad liquor in late 1926, Wayne Wheeler said, "The government is under no obligation to furnish the people with alcohol that is drinkable, when the Constitution prohibits it. The person who drinks this alcohol is a deliberate suicide." The wet Senator Edward Edwards (D-NJ) denounced the Anti-Saloon League lobbyist for condoning "murder." Wheeler's callousness fitted with the dry view that all alcohol was a poison. In 1930, there were 625 deaths from bad alcohol in New York City.

The safest way to supply America's thirst, it turned out, was to import alcohol. Cheap tequila and other distilled products made specifically for Americans crossed the porous Mexican border into Texas, Arizona, and California. "Texas will not be bone dry nor even approximate that state," concluded one journalist in 1922, "until Mexico, the great source of supply, takes the pledge." Alcohol tourists flooded Tijuana and other border towns. West Indian rum, Spanish and Portuguese wines and brandy, and Scots, Irish, and Canadian whiskey made its way, along with moonshine, via Nassau in the Bahamas to Texas, Louisiana, and Florida, the state with the longest coastline in the United States. Bellhops in Miami took liquor orders while escorting guests to their rooms. Scotch was $6.00 a quart, less than half the price in New York.

In the absence of beer, Americans wanted to replace domestic whiskey with a similar product. One possibility was Scotch, but Americans were not drawn to the smoky taste, the price was steep, the voyage was long, and getting large transatlantic ships past the US Coast Guard was hard. Trying to avoid antagonizing the United States government over prohibition, the British stopped direct shipments to America. In the earliest days of enforcement, the shipping industry believed that the Eighteenth Amendment did not apply outside the traditional three-mile limit. Passengers and crew drank while crossing the Atlantic. Then the Treasury Department declared that no ship that docked in the United States could carry alcohol inside the three-mile limit. After diplomatic protests, the State Department allowed foreign ships to enter American waters with alcohol on board so long as it was locked up. In return, the three-mile limit was extended to twelve miles. American ships, however, had to be bone dry. The travel industry was in turmoil, as Americans booked sailings on foreign vessels, and domestic lines vainly used games, films, or music as attractions to offset the loss of liquor.

Canadians generously stepped in to quench the thirst of their American neighbors. During the war Canada had imposed prohibition, and at the end of the war every province except Quebec remained dry. Canadian law allowed local distillers to make spirits for sale inside the United States so long as they paid a $20 per gallon export tax. Several large distilleries opened in Vancouver, British Columbia, to serve the West Coast. The liquor, however, was mediocre, and these export houses, as they were called, did not survive the end of prohibition. More successful was the major Ontario distillery Hiram Walker, which exported Canadian whiskey across the Detroit River into the Midwest. In 1922, one journalist estimated that one thousand cases a day crossed the river. In Saskatchewan, Samuel Bronfman, the son of Jewish immigrants from Eastern Europe, shipped spirits across the border to North Dakota. Realizing that the larger market was in the East, Bronfman moved to Montreal, constructed a giant distillery, and bought the firm of Seagram's. The House of Seagram both imported Scotch and made high-grade Canadian whiskey.

Some of Bronfman's liquor reached the Midwest through Detroit, but most of the product was shipped down the St. Lawrence River into the Atlantic Ocean, where Canadian vessels supplied dozens of mother ships that were anchored in international waters just beyond the three-mile limit of the United States. Collectively, these ships stretched from Cape Cod, Massachusetts, south to Norfolk, Virginia, and they became known as Rum Row. Small, fast vessels moved the liquor from Rum Row to the shore. After the limit was extended to twelve miles, one smuggler commented, "What is a mile or two extra? Now we have better and faster boats." This part of the East Coast was rich in coves and private beaches close to such major markets as Boston, New York, Philadelphia, Baltimore, and Washington. After goods were landed, they could also be transported by automobile caravans to Pittsburgh, Cleveland, or even as far west as Chicago.

Canadian liquor often arrived at the anchored ships in broad daylight, but the US Coast Guard legally could do nothing except watch it being unloaded. At night, speedboats that operated without lights darted from hidden spots along the coast to make a quick rendezvous with the anchored ships. Off-loadings were completed in minutes, and the speedboats reached shore long before the Coast Guard could do so. This was not an accident. The bootleggers had used public records to find out where the Coast Guard vessels had been built, they had gone to those shipyards and studied the blueprints, and then they had commissioned the same shipyards to build boats that were faster. Many speedboats used cheap surplus World War I aircraft engines. In 1925, the Prohibition Bureau estimated that only 5 percent of the liquor illegally entering the United States was stopped. The most famous rum-runner was Bill McCoy, who refused to cut liquor, honored business arrangements, and never cheated. His quality goods were labeled the Real McCoy, a brand of high reputation and premium price.

The most desirable coastal landing areas created opportunities for political corruption and graft. Atlantic City was a playground city a short distance from New York, a day trip by train or car. Long known as a place to drink, gamble, and score a prostitute, this beach mecca became a major landing spot to supply high-end liquor to the New York market. The resort was run by the Republican county treasurer Nucky Johnson and his brother, the sheriff. They demanded cash, which had to be spread around to any number of people, as well as a plentiful supply of alcohol to keep Atlantic City oiled for tourists and businessmen. At least some of the liquor sold there, however, was not Canadian whiskey, but the good stuff cut with second-rate local moonshine.

The tough men who ran illegal gambling and prostitution moved quickly to take over the liquor industry. The connection was natural, since drinking had often been associated with vice. In 1920–1921 John Torrio and his deputy, Al Capone, left New York, where they were minor racketeers, to move to Chicago. The pair rapidly took over prostitution and alcohol on the South Side. They brewed beer in a big way, while two hard liquor supply routes served Chicago. Using contacts in the New York underworld, they arranged for alcohol caravans from the East Coast and also bought spirits from the violent Purple Gang, which controlled the Detroit entry point.

In 1924, the most powerful mobster in Chicago, Dion O'Banion, the leader of the North Side gang, was murdered. With control of the Chicago beer market at stake, the North Side gang marked Torrio and Capone for death. After several bungled assassinations of both men, Torrio turned the business over to Capone, took $1 million and four guards to protect himself, and fled to Italy. By the late 1920s, Capone was the King of Beer in Chicago. He controlled breweries, employed one thousand people, paid off hundreds of elected officials and police, and supplied beer to twenty thousand speakeasies. Tied house took on a new meaning when a Capone lieutenant informed a speakeasy that it could carry only Capone's brand of beer. In 1926, Capone's organization grossed $70 million; three years later, it was $100 million, although the gang spent $30 million for protection in Chicago.

In 1929, Capone went too far. To get rid of the hated North Side gang, now run by Bugs Moran, and gain control of all the liquor and rackets in Chicago, Capone sent four hired guns, including two dressed as Chicago police, to kill the rival gang's leaders. Misidentifying one of the lieutenants as Moran, who was absent, the thugs invaded a meeting in a commercial garage. In what became known as the St. Valentine's Day massacre, the five rivals and two unfortunate witnesses were lined up in front of the cement wall inside the garage and machine-gunned to death with more than one thousand bullets. Afterward, Moran told the police, "Only Capone kills like that." He declined to say more then or later. Eventually, the police concluded that Capone and the Purple Gang were indeed involved. The Detroit gang supplied Capone, and Moran had tried to drop the Purples for a cheaper vendor. Although Moran survived, the death of his top aides ended the North Side gang, and Capone owned Chicago.

The massacre proved a miscalculation. The police were furious at the misuse of their uniforms. They had cooperated with the bootleggers, they resented being mocked, and misuse of uniforms jeopardized their lives. The newspapers printed horrific photographs that sold a lot of copies and jarred the public into disgust with the criminal underworld. *Little Caesar* (1931) and *Scarface* (1932) presented unflattering portraits of Capone on film, and the Federal Bureau of Investigation declared Capone to be Public Enemy No. 1. If there was any moment when the public turned against prohibition, it might have been this mass carnage. Prohibition did not stop drinking, but it did promote thugs like Capone, who both got rich and paid no taxes. Capone never recovered from being portrayed as a ruthless mass murderer. Prosecutors could not pin the crime on him, however, and when he finally was sent to prison in 1932, it was for federal income tax evasion. He was released in 1939, when he was dying from complications from untreated syphilis.

Not all bootleggers were like Capone. George Remus controlled alcohol in the greater Cincinnati area, which included parts of Ohio, Indiana, Kentucky, and West Virginia. The shrewd Chicago lawyer bought fourteen distilleries at the beginning of prohibition. Because distilling had been banned during the war, the sole value was in the inventory. Using political connections, Remus got rare permits to sell medicinal whiskey, to convert some spirits into industrial alcohol, and to distill additional industrial alcohol. Using fake permits and creative bookkeeping, he produced and sold far more spirits than his permits allowed, processed industrial alcohol into potable liquor, and supplied millions of gallons of spirits to drug stores and speakeasies throughout the region. He also owned breweries. Remus stored a large quantity of liquor at his farm near Cincinnati, and a federal raid in 1922 ended his career. To prevent confiscation, he turned his holdings over to his wife and went to prison. While he was in custody, she filed for divorce and took his money. After regaining his freedom, Remus had his revenge. In 1927, as his wife made her way to court to defend the divorce, he murdered her. The jury let him off, but she had already squandered the money.

In Seattle, Roy Olmstead, a former police lieutenant, controlled imports from Canada. Unlike other illegal operators, Olmstead insisted that his henchmen go unarmed. The business was conducted entirely with payoffs. Olmstead purchased liquor legally in Vancouver and had it loaded onto Canadian vessels along with proper export paperwork. These large ships traveled through the Strait of Juan de Fuca into international waters in the Pacific Ocean where spirits were transferred to smaller ships, some of which traveled as far south as southern California, although Olmstead never dominated the market outside Washington State. The small, fast ships brought liquor into Puget Sound, where cargo was dumped on deserted beaches to be picked up a few hours later by car caravans. The spirits were not cut with moonshine. Olmstead operated a radio station out of his Seattle mansion; his wife read children's bedtime stories on the air. The stories supposedly contained coded messages about the drop-off times and locations for the liquor.

Under the personally wet president Warren Harding, Prohibition Bureau agents were political hacks with little law enforcement experience. A good many had taught Methodist Sunday school, which was one way to get a recommendation from Wayne Wheeler of the Anti-Saloon League, and others were crooks or con artists who joined the bureau to get into the liquor racket. Agents could dispose of seized alcohol as they saw fit, and they often took spirits home to drink or sell. The bureau encouraged its agents to use violence. Seattle US attorney Tom Revelle told Senator Wesley Jones (R-WA), "Some of them [bootleggers] deserve a good killing, and I am not losing any sleep if now and then a bootlegger is killed." After Harding died in August 1923, President Calvin

Coolidge tried to reform the Prohibition Bureau. Because Wheeler refused to put federal agents under the civil service until 1927, reforms were modest, but one-third of the agents were dismissed for such matters as incompetence, theft, or alcoholism. At the time, the dry forces, probably still a majority in the country, wanted better enforcement.

Elected officials from the country's wettest states disagreed. Governor Albert Ritchie (D-MD) proposed that federal agents conduct raids only with the cooperation of local authorities. In effect, he wanted non-enforcement of prohibition in Maryland. In New York, the Anti-Saloon League had pushed the Mullan-Gage Act, a draconian state prohibition enforcement law, through the rural-dominated legislature in 1921, and the law had led to the defeat of the dry Republican governor Nathan Miller by the wet Democrat Al Smith the following year. An Irish Catholic, Smith had already served as governor from 1918 to 1920, when he had been defeated in the Harding landslide. Smith despised prohibition for the attack on personal liberty, the assault on immigrant cultures, and the loss of alcohol tax revenue, but he was also a personal wet who served alcohol in the governor's mansion in Albany.

In 1923, the newly wet New York legislature repealed the state's enforcement act. Under pressure from both sides, Smith hesitantly signed the bill, and after 1923 the only enforcement in the nation's most populous state came from the Prohibition Bureau. New York City had just 129 federal agents, though the US attorney estimated that 1,500 were necessary for effective enforcement of the law. From then on, dry Democrats considered Smith an enemy whose entire politics was defined by his wetness. William Jennings Bryan did not mince words: "When the governor of the largest state in the union boldly raises the black flag and offers to lead the representatives of the outlawed liquor traffic in their assault upon the nation's honor and the people's welfare, he must expect resistance from the defenders of the home, the school, and the church." Billy Sunday commented, "Governor Smith and that bunch of Tammany rough-necks can't ride into the White House on a wine keg or a barrel of beer."

In the 1924 election, Coolidge ran on the promise to improve prohibition enforcement, while the Democrats bitterly split at the national convention, held in New York, between the wet Smith and the dry William McAdoo of California, a former secretary of the treasury who was Woodrow Wilson's son-in-law. The most beloved Democrat, William Jennings Bryan, pressured delegates to reject Smith. If they backed Smith, the dry Bryan vowed to come into their state or district and campaign for a primary opponent. No elected Democrat wanted to face that prospect. Smith's supporters, however, were furious at the presence of the Ku Klux Klan at the convention. The Klan, which backed McAdoo, wanted a dry party; it was so powerful that the party defeated a proposal to condemn the Klan. The deadlocked convention compromised by ignoring prohibition and nominating the obscure conservative Wall Street attorney John W. Davis. Progressive Democrats bolted to the wet senator Robert LaFollette (R-WI), who ran on the Progressive Party ticket. Given the country's prosperity, neither Davis nor LaFollette had a chance, and the incumbent Coolidge won easily.

In Seattle, better enforcement in 1924 meant that federal agents put a wiretap on Roy Olmstead's telephone. Although Olmstead gave only cryptic instructions over the phone, the Prohibition Bureau raided Olmstead's house and took away his papers, which enabled them to develop a case. Olmstead's attorney assured his client that the wiretap, done without a court order, violated the Fourth Amendment, but the trial judge disagreed, and Olmstead was convicted in 1926. *Olmstead v. United States* (1927) went to the US Supreme Court, which voted 5–4 to uphold his conviction. There was to be no Fourth Amendment protection for bootleggers. Many constitutional lawyers condemned the decision, and Congress later passed a statute requiring a court order prior to any wiretap. In the 1920s the Supreme Court, led by Chief Justice William Howard Taft, routinely sided with the government in prohibition cases. Although Taft personally opposed prohibition, he hoped that the court's tough approach would force eventual repeal of the Eighteenth Amendment. If the court sided with bootleggers, the amendment would remain on the books, and liquor would stay untaxed.

Prohibition had led to other changes in the way alcohol was obtained and used. One way to get legal alcohol was to have a physician write a prescription for whiskey or beer, which many states allowed. These prescriptions turned drug stores into liquor stores. In 1916, Charles Walgreen owned nine pharmacies in Chicago, and by the end of the 1920s he operated 525. Legal alcohol profits enabled him to expand the empire quickly. A number of drug outlets, however, ignored federal recordkeeping; customers balked at being listed as liquor purchasers; or stores preferred to sell more profitable moonshine rather than the heavily taxed alcohol available from authorized distillers. A New York official told the *New York Times*, "When licenses to sell liquor for medicinal purposes were given to ex-saloonkeepers instead of to legitimate dispensers, the world knew we were not sincere." Though state law controlled the amount of alcohol that could be purchased at one time, patients could buy liquor from multiple stores. Physicians could write unlimited prescriptions, and druggists had a powerful incentive to maximize total sales.

Some saloons, restaurants, and hotel bars remained open throughout prohibition, but these older drinking establishments had been located to gain public notice; now that alcohol was illegal, they attracted too much attention. A few locked their doors and used back entrances. Some closed voluntarily; others were raided, padlocked, and ceased to operate. Of prewar licensed saloons in New York City, 80 percent were gone by 1924. The saloon tie to politics also ended. Under the Volstead Act, any building where liquor was sold could be seized by the federal government and padlocked for up to one year. In 1928, federal agents in Chicago closed seven hundred places. Landlords afraid of being padlocked often refused to rent to bootleggers. Accordingly, bootleggers often owned their own buildings, but they used dummy corporations to hide ownership. The loss of a place for a year was just a cost of doing business. A hotel, however, could not risk closure. Hotel bars mostly turned into tea rooms or retail space, and room prices rose. Famous gourmet restaurants, such as Delmonico's in New York, that had made their profit out of liquor sales went dry, lost customers, and were shuttered.

Drinking customers migrated to speakeasies and private clubs. Ranging from dangerous basement dives that sold unsafe industrial alcohol to upscale establishments like New York's 21 Club, which handled only the highest quality imported liquors at very high prices, speakeasies tried to meet the urban demand for alcohol. To be discreet, a typical speakeasy lacked any sign, and the large, thick, and plain wood door often contained either a peephole for the bouncer to see out or a small opening where the potential customer could be screened. Some "speaks" admitted only members or friends of members who knew the correct code words or had printed passes. Others took a chance on almost anyone who did not look like a federal agent. Local police officers were usually welcome. Their visibility tended to preserve order. "The first day we opened up the police came right in, four of them," recalled one New York speakeasy owner, "to be stood drinks, and I've had these four cops on my side in this business from that day on."

Unlike old-fashioned saloons, speakeasies admitted women. When both men and women entered the doorway, outsiders, including members of the Anti-Saloon League, were less likely to suspect that alcohol was being served. Décor and attractive male bartenders were used to draw women, who came alone, with friends, or with dates. The presence of couples discouraged fights. The author Stanley Walker observed, "Soon after 1920, raving

8. Art Janik opened his speakeasy in Milwaukee in 1931, but he also operated legally after repeal until 1937.

hordes of women began to discover what their less respectable sisters had known for years—that it was a lot of fun, if you liked it, to get soused." Harold Ross, editor of the *New Yorker*, was shocked at how much his star reporter, Lois Long, drank as she made the nightly rounds of speaks.

Female public drinking was associated with looser sexuality. In the 1920s, young women who wore short skirts, drank alcohol, and lived hedonistically were called flappers. *Variety* claimed that flappers were "as free with their persons…as a longshoreman." Of the flapper, Helen Lowry wrote in the *New York Times*, "She is the first woman in history that has not been checked at home when man went forth alone in search of his pleasures. And because of her we have with us the most merry, the least jaded night life yet." Freer sexuality may have led to a decline in prostitution. Many drinking houses expected barmaids to sell sex. In 1926, the old-fashioned moral reformers who belonged to the Committee of Fourteen found 360 of 392 speakeasies in New York harboring prostitutes, but skeptics doubted these numbers because it was hard to tell a prostitute from a woman expressing sexual liberation.

The *New Yorker*, launched in 1925, celebrated night life by promoting high-end nightclubs such as the Palais Royal, Moulin Rouge, Bal Tabarin, and Montmartre. Such clubs featured liquor, music, and dancing. Cabarets provided professional entertainment. New Yorkers had many choices, including bohemian cafes in Greenwich Village, mixed race "black and tan" spots in Harlem, and exclusive Fifth Avenue clubs. Nightclubs were lavishly decorated to encourage big spending, and they were expensive. Nightclubs projected an exclusive image but actually mixed different types of people, including wealthy stockbrokers, Broadway stars, celebrity writers, fashion models, flashy hucksters, scam artists, and sinister gangsters. "Never before has there ever been such a meeting ground of the very highest and the very lowest of human society," noted the *Smart Set* in 1927.

Harlem had many speakeasies and nightclubs. Ninety percent were white-owned and white-operated. Half of the rest were white-owned but run by African Americans, and the rest were black-owned and operated. Most were restricted either to white patrons, like the famous Cotton Club, or to blacks, but both races mingled in some places, which probably could not have occurred without prohibition. Breaking the racial taboo was as defiant as breaking the liquor law. Whites and blacks drank together, listened to jazz together, danced together, and occasionally slept together. Older black leaders in Harlem favored prohibition, opposed interracial nightclubs, and feared that the repeal of the Eighteenth Amendment might lead to the repeal of the Thirteenth Amendment abolishing slavery, but young African American writers like Langston Hughes frequented Harlem speaks.

While whites used Harlem as a playground, poor black residents were regulars at neighborhood hootch joints or rent parties. Because rents were high in Harlem, and because few African Americans had good jobs, paying rent was always a problem. Resourceful tenants temporarily removed furniture from their apartments to hold a party with free food, music, and space for dancing. Guests paid a small admission charge, which went toward the rent. Patrons brought their own alcohol or bought small amounts at the party. Some tenants held rent parties every week, particularly on weekend nights. To attract guests, operators passed out handbills on the sidewalk, called down from windows, or simply allowed jazz to waft through the neighborhood. Only African Americans were welcome at these events. Because the Prohibition Bureau had very few black agents, a raid was unlikely.

A few owners or operators of speaks became famous. None was more colorful than Texas Guinan, a silent screen star who left California to run a speakeasy in New York. She had grown up in Texas, loved to ride horses, played vaudeville, and became America's first film cowgirl. At her nightclub, Tex knew how to put on a show. She fondly greeted regular customers by name, tried to cheer up those who seemed depressed, and emphasized that having a good time was more important than drinking, which was just a way to get started on having a good time. She had a big heart. Once, when the journalist Heywood Hale Broun tried to impress his girlfriend by ordering an overpriced bottle of bad champagne, Tex insisted that he buy a regular drink. Later, she told him that she knew his weekly salary, and she had no intention of letting a regular like him go bankrupt on champagne designed for out-of-town suckers.

Drinking also took place discreetly in ice cream stores, soft drink shops, beauty parlors, and funeral homes. Another new type of watering hole in the twenties was the roadhouse, as rising automobile ownership enabled drivers to enjoy liquor out of town. Customers were not likely to be seen, which made these highway resorts good for a tryst. Disguised as restaurants, roadhouses often provided elegant meals, a romantic atmosphere, danceable music, perhaps gambling, a few rooms available to rent for the night, and maybe even discreet prostitution. Other roadhouses were abandoned barns. Federal raids were unlikely, and payoffs were lower than in cities because there were fewer people to silence. The liquor was usually inexpensive, but it might be unreliable moonshine made on the premises.

A lot of drinking took place at home because the law allowed domestic production of fruit wine or cider. A head of household could ferment up to two hundred gallons of fruit juice a year for family use. Grape juice, sugar, and yeast were the only necessary ingredients. California vintners shipped Alicante grapes to make wine, but they also dried grapes, pressed them into bricks, and sold them to make reconstituted grape juice. Vino Sano Grape Brick came with instructions to add water to make juice but warned that sugar and yeast would create an alcoholic beverage. Brick sales soared. The wet editor Arthur Brisbane promoted Vine-Glo: "The Grape Growers are not held responsible for the laws of nature, which seem to have no sympathy for Prohibition, and turn innocent Grape Juice into Wine." Or perhaps one knew a rabbi or Catholic priest, real or fake, who might provide wine in return for a contribution. Home spirits distillation was riskier, because even a small amount of untaxed moonshine could bring a stiff fine, jail time, and possible confiscation of real estate.

One could buy moonshine, but amateur distillers tended to be ignorant and poorly educated. Some moonshine was poisonous redistilled industrial alcohol, and some was equally poisonous wood alcohol. Not every producer knew or cared that the use of a car radiator as a still was dangerous because the lead contaminated the liquor. To mask moonshine's bad taste, flavorings were added, including Jamaican ginger extract, which led to the product called "jake." Much of what was sold as jake was poisonous. It might kill, or it could cripple the victim, causing what was called jake leg. In 1930, fifty thousand poor people in Kansas City, Oklahoma City, and Cincinnati were paralyzed. For home consumption, it was best to buy from a reputable bootlegger. Finding such a vendor was difficult, but once found, the customer treasured the seller. The youthful writer Bernard DeVoto supplied the Harvard faculty with liquor. A master of the back roads in Vermont, he bought excellent liquors and French wines in Montreal before evading US Customs to slip back into the United States.

Because the safest place to drink without being arrested was at home, the middle class invented the home cocktail party. Hostesses issued written invitations, and dress was often formal. Cocktails were modern and sophisticated, and women found taking a mixed drink to be an adventure. Because the mediocre bootleg spirits had to be cut with a mixer to be palatable, the hostess prepared cocktails in the kitchen and then passed them around the living room on a tray. Men drank martinis and Manhattans, while women took sweeter drinks such as gin fizzes or lime rickeys. Both drank highballs: liquor with club soda, tonic water, or ginger ale served in a tall glass over ice. The *New Yorker* published street prices for alcohol as well as recipes for mixed drinks. Fashionable stores sold serving trays, cocktail shakers, tall highball glasses, and stirring sticks. Canapés were also provided, but at many parties the purpose was to get smashed. The question was which gave out first, the liquor or the guests.

House parties could be grand affairs. The owner of a mansion might entertain hundreds of guests, many of whom he had never met. They were not friends but people who had heard that there was a party, knew that alcohol would be available, and owned an automobile to get there. The bootlegger George Remus loved to entertain this way in Cincinnati, although he frequently got bored and retreated to his library to read a book. The fictional Jay Gatsby also held big parties at his house on Long Island Sound. "The fashionable rich," complained the *Ladies Home*

Journal in 1923, "demand their rum as an inalienable class privilege." So did the middle class. In the Sinclair Lewis novel *Babbitt* (1922), real estate broker George Babbitt and his middle-class friends drank cocktails while endorsing prohibition for the working class.

The class bias of prohibition was extraordinary. The Yale Club legally served prewar alcohol to its members, but working-class speakeasies were raided. "It makes for hypocrisy and class hatred," said the *New York World*. Louis Swift, the wealthy Chicago meatpacker, told a journalist that prohibition was good for the working class. He held a cocktail in his hand as he made the remark. Speaks near factories were closed when employers tipped the Prohibition Bureau. Lillian Wald, founder of the Henry Street Settlement, defended prohibition despite the class bias. Workers used to spend entire paychecks in saloons; now they bought consumer goods. Small-town drys cared only about the drinking of Catholic and Jewish immigrants and African Americans who were either working class or poor. Wets were, accordingly, "un-American." Before prohibition, drys had denounced the saloon for victimizing the drinker. Now they denounced the drinker for defying the Constitution. "If they do not like the way things are being done," advised the Methodist Board of Temperance, "let them go back to Europe."

Youth drinking was another feature of the 1920s. Elders were alarmed that young men and women drank together. To the young, who had missed the moral zeal of the Progressive Era, the idea of prohibition seemed bizarre and unfair. In 1926, a poll found that four-fifths of Yale University students opposed prohibition; nearly half favored a government alcohol monopoly. One Columbia University student observed, "They say we should cultivate respect for the prohibition law because they fixed it so it can't be repealed. Queer reason for respecting a law!" Drinking was just one way young Americans rebelled. Flappers talked dirty, bobbed their hair, wore short skirts, put on lipstick, and carried flasks in their boots. The automobile made a love nest for premarital sex, which was contemplated and discussed even if uncommon. Much of what happened in the twenties was a youthful show put on to shock strait-laced older people. There was quite a bit of play acting.

Through self-promotion, the Prohibition Bureau agents Izzy Einstein and Moe Smith frequently made the *New York Times*. Einstein was a natural actor, and he loved faking his identity to catch liquor violators. He appeared to care less about prohibition and more about being able to con crooks. At one time or another he pretended to be a rabbi, a violinist, a fisherman, a baseball player, an ice man, and an undertaker. His victims fell for his phony lines and tried to sell Einstein liquor, whereupon the game was up. In 1925, jealous superiors fired Einstein and Smith. Another publicity hound was Eliot Ness of the Untouchables, an elite unit of the Prohibition Bureau that had been hand-picked for being free of corruption. Ness vied with Internal Revenue for taking credit for ending Capone's career.

The chief enforcer in the United States was Mabel Walker Willebrandt, who was the highest-ranking woman in the federal government. Before prohibition she drank alcohol, but she believed in law enforcement. From 1921 to 1928, she was the assistant attorney general in the Justice Department in charge of liquor prosecutions. Early on, she realized that enforcement funds were inadequate, that there were too few agents, that small fry were arrested while powerful gangsters were ignored due to lack of local police cooperation. She disapproved of the wiretap in the Olmstead case. In 1928, Willebrandt strongly backed the dry Herbert Hoover for president. She had known Hoover from her days in California, and she hoped that his enforcement would be more energetic than Coolidge's. A vigorous campaigner among dry women's groups, she expected to be named attorney general. Hoover won, but she was not nominated. She returned to California to practice law, and in 1930 she became the top lawyer

9. Mlle. Rhea, a vaudeville entertainer, displayed the latest garter flask while on tour in Washington, DC, in 1926.

for the California Fruit Growers Coop, which produced grape concentrate to make wine.

The politics of alcohol began to change during Coolidge's presidency. Better enforcement had failed to dry out the cities, and gang wars had become more violent. By the mid-1920s, growing numbers of Americans questioned the wisdom of prohibition. In 1926, Al Smith sponsored a referendum in New York State calling for modification, which won by a 3 to 1 margin. The Woman's Christian Temperance Union, under the leadership of Ella Boole, seemed out of touch with public opinion when it demanded tougher penalties, and the Anti-Saloon League lost much of its power when Wayne Wheeler died suddenly in August 1927. Wheeler was a lawyer, a brilliant lobbyist, and a subtle political strategist who understood how to keep Congress on the dry side. The Ohio Republican resisted actions that he thought would undermine prohibition. To Wheeler, the law worked well enough in small-town America that it deserved to remain in place. He was optimistic that education and proper assimilation of immigrants to the standards that he espoused would dry out the cities in another generation.

Wheeler insisted that prohibition not become a partisan issue. If one party went wet, the wet party might eventually gain power and destroy prohibition. To prevent that result, dry majorities were needed in both parties. After Wheeler died, the ASL's Washington lobbyist was James Cannon, the Methodist bishop of Virginia. Not only was Cannon a moralist blind to political complexities, but he was also an ardent southern Democrat. His lack of influence with the Republican majority in Congress weakened the ASL, and his strident demand that the Democratic Party be dry clashed with the growing influence of wet urban Democrats inside the party. Booming industrial cities in the 1920s were beginning to tilt power in that direction. The ten most populous cities grew by 24 percent in the 1920s, when the entire country gained only 16 percent. Urban growth was concentrated in wet New York, Chicago, and Detroit.

In 1924 and 1926, Al Smith easily won two new two-year terms as governor of the battleground state of New York, the most populous state, and in 1928 he ran for president a second time. William Jennings Bryan had died in 1925, which put dry forces at the Democratic National Convention on the defensive. Party leaders saw Smith as the strongest candidate. To placate Bishop Cannon and the dry southerners, the platform was wishy-washy on prohibition. Smith was nominated with the understanding, arranged by party leaders, that he would downplay the issue. The nominee, however, was a product of New York City's Tammany Hall, a political machine rooted in saloons. Just before the convention adjourned, Smith announced that he favored modifying the Volstead Act to allow beer or beer and light wine. He shrugged off saloons as "defunct." Excluding brief stays at the governor's mansion in Albany, the parochial Smith had never lived anywhere except New York City. In supporting alcohol, he spoke from the heart, and no doubt most of the city's residents agreed with him. To dry southerners, however, he had betrayed the convention agreement, and he seemed to be sneering at ignorant rural hicks.

Then Smith dropped the bombshell that the head of the Democratic National Committee would be John Raskob, a former Republican donor, a General Motors executive, a militant wet, and a fellow Roman Catholic. Indeed, Smith and Raskob had met through service at Catholic charities. The appointment signaled that Smith was pro-business, and the party chair raised so much money that the Democrats outspent the Republicans, which was unusual. Raskob feared federal power and wanted the Democrats to be a wet business party. The executive was close to Pierre du Pont, another wet business leader who had organized the Association Against the Prohibition Amendment (AAPA) with the insight that income taxes on the rich could be reduced if prohibition was repealed. Many southern Democrats despised northern capitalists, liked income taxes, and regarded drinking as the bane of the urban masses. Those southerners found Smith's views and actions galling, even before they considered the religious dimension.

Given the recent activity of the anti-Catholic Ku Klux Klan, it was hard to see how Smith's religion was not going to be an issue in 1928. In the North, where most rural Protestants were Republicans, the issue was not important, but rural dry southern Democrats who disliked Smith as an urban wet could not help but play the religious card. Bishop Cannon wanted to teach his party not to take the South for granted. He had no use for a wet Democratic Party. "I have been fighting the liquor traffic all my life," he wrote Bishop Warren Candler of Georgia. Smith's wet Catholicism led Cannon to back the dry Quaker, Herbert Hoover, and Cannon's power was such that Virginia voted Republican. Smith also lost North Carolina, Florida, Tennessee, and Texas, as well as the border states of West Virginia, Kentucky, and Oklahoma. Although the loss was later seen as proof of widespread anti-Catholicism, most commentary at the time stressed Smith's liquor stand as the key to his southern debacle.

Smith did gain wet-urban-Catholic votes in the North, mostly from immigrants who registered and voted for the first time. From 1896 to 1924, with the exception of Wilson's first election, Republicans had carried the country's twelve most populous cities, but the great wet cities voted Democratic in 1928. Smith won the customarily Republican wet states of Massachusetts and Rhode Island on a tide of new voters. The Republican vote in both states remained the same, but the Democratic vote soared. In Chicago, 61 percent of Smith's voters had never before cast ballots. Smith also carried his native New York City, but not by enough to overcome the dry Republican majority in rural upstate New York. While the militantly wet Smith lost his home state and thereby forfeited any chance to be the party's nominee a second time, his protégé, Franklin D. Roosevelt, who waffled on prohibition, got more upstate votes, narrowly won the New York governorship, and emerged as a strong presidential contender for 1932.

Waffling captured the public mood in 1928. Coolidge's pledge to improve enforcement had failed in areas where wet defiance was commonplace. In 1920, there were 1,520 federal agents; ten years later, 2,836. During the 1920s, New York City had thirty thousand speakeasies and nightclubs. The Prohibition Bureau budget had increased from $4.75 million in 1921 to $12.4 million in 1929, but it did not seem to matter. Federal and local courts were clogged with liquor cases, and routine business cases were caught in the jam. In the federal courts in New York City, prohibition cases were two-thirds of criminal cases from 1920 to1922. Plea bargaining, new to federal court, became rampant, and Volstead Act violators usually got off with small fines. There was little interest in sending moonshiners or bootleggers to prison, which cost taxpayer money. The fines, however, made up for the loss of alcohol taxes. Courts scheduled bargain days, where hundreds of violators who pleaded guilty to lesser charges in mass proceedings paid their fines immediately.

The wet state of Maryland had never passed an enforcement statute, so the only prohibition cases in the Free State were in federal court, but the number of Prohibition Bureau agents was insufficient to make even a small dent in the Baltimore liquor traffic. By 1929, the states of Massachusetts, Wisconsin, and Montana had joined New York in repealing state dry statutes, and so, they, too, lacked state enforcement. States spent little on enforcement; in 1927 twenty-eight states spent nothing. In Virginia, dry laws were mainly used by politically connected bootleggers to ruin competitors or to harass poor whites and African Americans who tried to sell liquor. In California, enforcement depended on county prosecutors. In wet San Francisco, the district attorney brought only a few cases; in Los

Angeles, police ignored major bootleggers but arrested many Mexican Americans who sold small amounts of alcohol.

Although Hoover won the 1928 election largely thanks to prosperity, he also played the prohibition card. Raised as a dry Quaker, Hoover was married to a prohibitionist, but his record was not that of a teetotaler. He did not believe 2.75 percent beer was intoxicating, he had opposed wartime prohibition, and he had once owned an excellent wine cellar. While secretary of commerce in the 1920s he had sometimes stopped for a cocktail at the Belgian embassy, which was wet foreign soil. Like many moderates, he did not necessarily see legal compulsion as the best solution to the liquor problem. He was deeply offended by the rise of organized crime among bootleggers, and in 1928 he supported the Anti-Saloon League's call for better enforcement. The dry forces believed that Hoover's election had been a referendum on prohibition and that they had won a convincing victory. In early 1929, the ASL asked Congress to increase the number of Prohibition Bureau agents, but conservative Republicans in Congress opposed any increase in government spending. Members may also have sensed a lack of public support for more agents.

As a substitute for more agents, Senator Wesley Jones (R-WA), one of the ASL leaders in Congress, introduced a bill to increase penalties for violating the Volstead Act. Whereas the old law called for first offenders to receive a prison term of six months and a maximum fine of $1,000, the new statute, called the Jones Act, imposed five years and $10,000 for a first offense. In addition, possession of alcohol in a speakeasy became a federal crime. A customer who failed to report any illegal sale that he had witnessed could be charged with a felony. Coolidge signed the "five and dime" law as his term expired. Harsh penalties were supposed to end moonshining and bootlegging, but prosecutors disliked the Jones Act. Plea bargains became more difficult, which further clogged the courts, and jurors in wet areas resisted convicting violators when jurors felt that the punishment was extreme.

Facing mounting criticism over the failure of enforcement, including public reaction to the St. Valentine's Day massacre, Hoover appointed a commission headed by the respected attorney George Wickersham to ponder national law enforcement policies. The Wickersham Commission took testimony for two years. The evidence overwhelmingly showed that prohibition was not being enforced and realistically could not be enforced short of creating a national police state. Few Americans liked that idea. The Prohibition Bureau was corrupt and incompetent, and the idea of joint federal-state law enforcement failed whenever the two sets of officials operated under different principles, political constraints, and legal systems. Federal prisoners rose from three thousand in 1915 to twelve thousand in 1930; one-third were liquor violators. State prisons were similarly crowded.

In 1931, the Wickersham Commission was ready to report, but the group was badly split. Nine of eleven members stated that the public did not support the Eighteenth Amendment. Nevertheless, five wanted to pursue better enforcement, while six called prohibition unworkable. Of this latter group, four wanted to modify the Volstead Act to allow beer and light wine, and two urged repeal of the Eighteenth Amendment, which was politically impossible in 1931. Forewarned about the split and alarmed by how his dry backers would react, Hoover demanded that the report unanimously stress better enforcement. Privately, he called the report "rotten." The original split, however, was leaked to the press, and Hoover's emphasis on enforcement sounded limp. For two years the administration had awaited a report that blandly embraced failed policies; the report made the government look inept. Even without the Great Depression, Hoover was in deep political trouble because of the failure of prohibition.

By 1931, the dry movement had produced decidedly mixed results. The politically crooked, vice-ridden saloon was dead, and overall drinking was reduced. In the early 1920s, per capita alcohol consumption may have dropped by two-thirds from its prewar level, but it rebounded later in the decade until it was about one-third below the prewar rate. Much of the lower consumption during prohibition was due to the high price of alcohol, which particularly affected working-class drinkers. The generation that came of age at that time drank little in later years, and per capita alcohol consumption did not regain its prewar peak until 1973. At the same time, prohibition had failed to dry out America, as supporters had promised that it would. In mid-decade, prohibitionists believed that the dry dream would be realized if only more effort was put into the cause. Thirst, however, never ceased, and allowing thugs like Al Capone to murder and rob to supply liquor seemed like a dubious price to pay for pursuing what Hoover had called the "noble" experiment. Nobility and Capone were words unlikely to be linked. Then there was the matter of the lost taxes, not just Capone's untaxed millions but the amounts that could be raised from alcohol taxes and license fees. As the Great Depression worsened, government revenues slumped at all levels, demand for public services increased, and the possibility of alcohol revenues became increasingly attractive.

Chapter 4
Repeal

Organized opposition to prohibition crystallized even before the Eighteenth Amendment went into effect. In 1918, irate business leaders founded the Association Against the Prohibition Amendment (AAPA). These wealthy conservatives drank socially; they opposed high personal income taxes, disliked federal police power, and worried about greater regulation of business. The AAPA wanted to replace income taxes with alcohol taxes, but this goal had little appeal except among the rich. In the early 1920s, the AAPA shoveled campaign contributions to wet politicians to offset the Anti-Saloon League's contributions to dry politicians, but they had indifferent results. This elite organization restricted membership to significant donors, such as the chemical corporate executive Pierre du Pont and his top aide John Raskob. The AAPA's *Freedom* magazine was circulated to leading country clubs in the East. Membership was 150,000 in 1930. In contrast, Al Smith's wetness was rooted in mass appeal and his close ties to Tammany Hall, the corrupt Democratic political machine that ran New York City. When Raskob joined Smith's campaign, he was unable to bring along many AAPA leaders. They were wealthy Republicans who did not fully trust anyone tied to Tammany Hall.

Throughout the twenties, the Republican Party was identified with prohibition, but two prominent wet Republicans undercut that image. Nicholas Murray Butler, the president of Columbia

University, gave the wet cause a respectable champion who was a formidable public debater. Representative Fiorello La Guardia, a wet reformer from East Harlem, constantly ridiculed the Prohibition Bureau, which raided his poor Italian immigrant constituents while ignoring wealthy drinkers who frequented fancy clubs. He held a press conference in his Capitol Hill office at which he demonstrated how to mix near-beer with flavored malt tonic to make homemade beer. He also argued that 2.75 percent beer should be legal. La Guardia taunted law enforcement to arrest him for making beer, but no one took the bait.

By the late 1920s, Americans increasingly recognized that prohibition could not work, but getting the political system to tackle the issue was hard. Part of the problem was a three-way split: In 1930 an unscientific *Literary Digest* mail-in poll of 4.8 million respondents showed 30 percent backed prohibition, 29 percent favored modifying the Volstead Act to bring back beer or beer and light wine, and 40 percent wanted to repeal the Eighteenth Amendment. Nevertheless, the shift against prohibition was clear. In 1930, members of the American Bar Association voted 2 to 1 for repeal. Wet converts included Alfred P. Sloan Jr., president of General Motors, and the billionaire John D. Rockefeller Jr., who had financially backed the Anti-Saloon League. Rockefeller's recantation in June 1932, just before the Republican National Convention, made big news. He argued that prohibition had to go to save civilization from outlaws. The American Legion, Veterans of Foreign Wars, and the American Federation of Labor also backed repeal.

Savvy politicians estimated that it would take a decade to organize a successful campaign to repeal the amendment, and some doubted that it could be done at all, considering the way rural America dominated the state legislatures that were required for ratification of a new constitutional amendment. As late as September 1930, the dry senator Morris Sheppard (D-TX), author of the Eighteenth Amendment, boasted, "There is as much chance of repealing the Eighteenth Amendment as there is for a hummingbird to fly to the planet Mars with the Washington Monument tied to its tail." Few people disagreed. If prohibition had been created by the national crisis of World War I, it would take another national crisis, the Great Depression that began in 1929, to end prohibition. As the economy declined in the early thirties, government officials at all levels faced falling revenues while the demand for public services increased. This appetite for revenue, along with changing public opinion, forced reconsideration of alcohol policy. In early 1932, the *Literary Digest* reported that 73 percent of 4.7 million mail-in ballots wanted to end prohibition; Americans who had previously favored modification now embraced repeal.

Language also mattered. The AAPA's problem was clarity: what the organization opposed was clear, but it lacked any specific plan to replace prohibition. In the 1920s, few Americans favored the return of the raunchy, prewar all-male saloon, and the formerly powerful brewers remained in disrepute. Many people would have been satisfied with home or restaurant use of legal beer or beer and light wine. Whiskey had few friends, because it had been associated with vice, wife beating, child abuse, and public drunkenness. To oppose prohibition was to promote a negative idea, which seldom works in politics. To rally support, a campaign for positive change was needed. Only in the late twenties did opponents begin to describe what they wanted by using the word "repeal." Repeal was a catch-all concept that linked those who favored saloons to those who preferred only retail sale of beer and wine for home use to those who desired tight government controls on alcohol. As a positive concept, repeal offered several possible wet visions distinct from the dry paradise imagined by prohibitionists.

Pauline Sabin, the wife of a wealthy Wall Street banker, decided to act. Mrs. Charles Sabin, as she was known socially, entered politics when women gained the vote. In 1920, she had believed in prohibition, and she had worked strenuously for the election of Warren Harding as president. Harding's corrupt and mediocre Prohibition Bureau had disenchanted Sabin, but in 1924 she campaigned for Calvin Coolidge with his promise of better enforcement. During the twenties, Sabin served as the Republican national committeewoman from New York, one of the highest party offices open to a woman at that time. In 1928, she backed Herbert Hoover, but she did so with the hope that Hoover would recognize the failure of enforcement. After the election, she quickly gave up on Hoover as an agent of change. Hoover's wife was dry, and he had been elected with the open support of the ASL and the Woman's Christian Temperance Union, so perhaps he was incapable of adopting any new policy.

Sabin's own views about prohibition shifted during the twenties. She and her husband lived in a twenty-eight-room oceanfront mansion on Long Island. The house had a built-in vault used as an alcohol repository. She served exquisite liquors and fine wines, all bought legally before prohibition, at their frequent dinner parties. Sabin herself was a light drinker. Guests often included members of Congress, who rarely turned down a drink, even while they explained that they continued to support both the Eighteenth Amendment and the Volstead Act. The hypocrisy infuriated Sabin. In addition, she worried that her two adolescent sons would be enticed into drinking deadly moonshine. Sabin decided to attack prohibition in order to end hypocrisy and to save her sons.

An educated, gracious, poised, and articulate woman who had a magnificent radio voice, Sabin began to campaign for repeal in 1929. "There was a large group ready to be organized, wanting to be organized," she later recalled. To attract attention and rally support, she created the Women's Organization for National Prohibition Reform (WONPR). She used lists from the Red Cross, the League of Women Voters, and the Parent-Teacher Association to recruit local leaders. An inclusive organization, WONPR welcomed Democrats, Republicans, Independents, women of all races, wealthy society women, middle-class housewives, and union leaders. To gain support, Sabin argued, "Telling citizens what they must or must not do in their strictly personal conduct, as long as public safety is not affected, is a function which the government should not attempt."

For decades, the WCTU had claimed that all women supported prohibition. After women started voting in 1920, elected officials avoided offending the WCTU, which might mobilize a massive bloc of women opposing them at the next election. Playing upon this fear, Ella Boole, the president of the WCTU, testified before Congress in 1928, "I represent the women of America." Boole's claim offended Sabin. "Well, lady," she recalled thinking, "here's one woman you don't represent." Unlike the upper-class Sabin, Boole, the wife of a Methodist minister, was middle class. The two women exchanged a number of radio barbs, which enhanced the visibility of the WONPR and undercut Boole's claim that she represented all American women. Boole then retreated to the older WCTU line, which was that she represented all respectable women. Clarence True Wilson of the Methodist Board of Temperance called the WONPR a "little group of wine-drinking society women." Sabin's radio addresses, however, showed that she was not empty-headed, and she never drank in public, so the WCTU looked foolish.

A superb organizer, Sabin used radio, public speeches, magazine articles, and mass mailings to reach her audience. Rallying millions of younger urban women, she asked them to join WONPR and to help sign up new recruits; by 1930, the organization claimed 400,000 members. The WCTU, in contrast, was in decline; under Ella Boole it had sunk to 381,000 members. WONPR continued to grow and topped 1 million in 1933. The large size of Sabin's group gave cover to politicians who had long recognized that prohibition had failed. "When women entered the fight for repeal," Al Smith noted, "sanity began to return to the country." Elected officials who opposed prohibition often used

Sabin's arguments. WONPR cited hypocrisy, lost revenue, bootlegger thugs, and dangerous illicit alcohol. When queried, politicians frequently said that America's women had caused them to change their views.

No longer terrified of the WCTU, numerous candidates for Congress in 1930 promised either to legalize beer and light wine or to repeal the Eighteenth Amendment and return the issue to the states. Surveying the election results, Sabin accurately called the 1930 midterm election a wet landslide, which in turn helped WONPR gain even more support. "I know of nothing since the days of the campaign for woman's suffrage," Sabin said in 1931, "to equal the campaign which women are now conducting for repeal of the Eighteenth Amendment." To avoid the charge that it favored saloons or drunkenness, the WONPR stressed that it wanted rigorous government regulation of the alcohol industry. By 1932, Sabin was determined to use the WONPR to support a wet presidential candidate regardless of party.

Franklin Delano Roosevelt, that most masterful of politicians, had narrowly won election as governor of New York in 1928. He was no friend of Tammany Hall, and the New York City machine had given him only tepid support, while it pushed Al Smith for president. In the summer of 1928, Eleanor Roosevelt, a committed dry whose father and brother had died of alcoholism, campaigned among upstate dry groups, and Franklin Roosevelt benefited from the support of progressive Republicans who had backed Eleanor's uncle Teddy in earlier years. As governor, Roosevelt forced out the corrupt Tammany-backed mayor, Jimmy Walker, who was replaced with a wet Republican reformer who backed Roosevelt, Fiorello La Guardia. Bootleggers had a lot to do with Walker's corruption. Tammany vowed to back Smith over Roosevelt for the 1932 presidential nomination, which deprived the new governor of his large home-state delegation. Facing reelection in 1930, Roosevelt dodged prohibition as much as possible. He said that he favored law enforcement, a hollow promise considering that

Repeal

Smith had repealed New York's state enforcement law in 1923. Roosevelt won reelection.

As the economy worsened, Governor Roosevelt passed imaginative social programs, and to pay for them, he was prepared to raise taxes. Roosevelt also moved to line up backing around the country for the presidential nomination in 1932. To win that nomination, he needed strong support from southern delegations in states where drys were strong. While the other Democratic candidates called for repeal, Roosevelt remained wishy-washy in early 1932, and Eleanor continued to speak to dry groups. Whenever Franklin Roosevelt was asked about prohibition, he stressed that the economy was a far more important issue. He believed that the Great Depression required federal action. His activist policies as governor suggested that he was serious.

When the Democratic National Convention opened in Chicago in June 1932, Roosevelt was the leading candidate, but he lacked the two-thirds vote needed to win the nomination. His managers found that unless the governor took a wetter position on alcohol, his candidacy was doomed. The delegates had already emptied five thousand liquor bottles. Finally, Roosevelt won the nomination when the wet John Nance Garner delivered the Texas delegation in return for the vice presidency, and the formerly dry but now wet newspaper publisher William Randolph Hearst delivered the California delegation in return for a promise to repeal prohibition. In an unprecedented gesture, Roosevelt stunned the convention and the country by accepting the nomination in person. He said, "This convention wants repeal. Your candidate wants repeal. And I am confident that the United States of America wants repeal." The delegates roared their approval. This reaction marked the high point of his acceptance speech.

Although the economy was the main issue in the campaign, Roosevelt also seized the opportunity to mobilize wet support across party lines. He promised to repeal both the Volstead Act

and the Eighteenth Amendment. Elected officials generally
supported the idea because it promised to curb organized crime,
reduce corruption, and enable governments at all levels to gain
badly needed alcohol license fees and tax revenues. In the South, a
number of formerly dry politicians suddenly followed their
constituents by switching sides. Pauline Sabin, a lifelong
Republican, made front page news when the WONPR endorsed
Roosevelt. Hoover, running for a second term, was left with
defending a record of failed enforcement by promising that
unspecified changes would be made. Thanks to the Great
Depression, Roosevelt won in a landslide. He carried wet
Templeton, Iowa, 446 to 14. In 1933, the town voted to repeal
Iowa's prohibition law 403 to 11.

Shortly after the election, James Farley, one of Roosevelt's key
aides and, as postmaster general, the main dispenser of patronage
in the new administration, announced that any Democrat who did
not support repeal of both the Volstead Act and the Eighteenth
Amendment would receive no patronage. Many new wets had
been elected not only to Congress but also to state legislatures.
The House had at least 343 wet members; the Senate, 61. At the
same November 1932 election in which Roosevelt had won,
Washington State voters had dumped Senator Wesley Jones
(R-WA), author of the draconian Jones Act, and had passed an
initiative repealing all the state's prohibition laws except one
restricting the drinking age to twenty-one. Eight other states had
voted to end state prohibition or enforcement. While dry
Democrats in the South such as Bishop James Cannon railed
against the trend, elected Democratic officials cultivated the new
administration. Amid 25 percent unemployment, patronage jobs
were even more important than usual, and all Democrats in
Congress wanted to be seen as supportive of Roosevelt in order to
receive federal help for their states or districts.

Roosevelt knew that legalizing alcohol was a concrete action
that could easily be taken early in the administration. The Great

Depression was a far more difficult problem, experts disagreed about how it should be handled, and the economic issues could not be quickly solved in any case. Meanwhile, Roosevelt could get Congress to modify the Volstead Act to allow legal beer, and he could start on the more difficult task of repealing the Eighteenth Amendment. Moreover, legal beer would increase the pressure to repeal the amendment, and the early availability of beer would enhance Roosevelt's reputation as an effective political leader. Most likely to be impressed were urban working-class drinkers who had often failed to vote in the past. Legal beer would demonstrate that Roosevelt, despite his upper-class origins, was a true friend of the working class and not just a member of the elite who sought working-class votes on Election Day.

The outgoing Congress decided to enact the Twenty-First Amendment, repealing the Eighteenth, even before Roosevelt was inaugurated. After an attempt to pass the wet amendment failed narrowly in the House in December 1932, the Senate considered a slightly different measure in early 1933. Senator Morris Sheppard mounted an ineffective filibuster, and the amendment, which did not require any action from outgoing President Herbert Hoover, passed the Senate, 63–23. "The taxpayer has paid the police to catch the bootlegger," declared Representative William Oliver (D-AL), "and has turned around and paid the bootlegger to evade the police. It's time we made his money count for something." On February 20, the House voted 289–121 to send the measure to the states for ratification. The new amendment turned over management of alcohol to the states with the exception that the federal government pledged to stop interstate sales into any state where state law barred such sales.

The United Repeal Council, headed by Pierre du Pont, had studied repeal in depth. The council was a temporary alliance of the AAPA, WONPR, the Crusaders, the American Hotel Association, and the Voluntary Committee of Lawyers. The American Legion and American Federation of Labor also collaborated with the council. Acting on the advice of the lawyers, the council insisted that the Twenty-First Amendment not be sent to state legislatures for ratification because of the fear that rural majorities in some legislatures might block ratification. "Thirteen dry states with a population of less than that of New York State alone," noted the wet attorney Clarence Darrow, "can prevent repeal." Instead, Congress decided to send the amendment to state ratifying conventions. Special elections to select convention delegates provided the opportunity for voters to express their views on prohibition.

Aided by the AAPA and WONPR, Postmaster Farley used patronage and party workers to push for speedy elections and to get out the vote. Congress had created one other form of pressure when it had passed temporary federal income and excise tax surcharges; these measures were set to expire automatically if repeal won. Experts estimated that repeal would raise $500 million annually in federal alcohol taxes and an equal amount in state and local revenues. The legal alcohol industry would create 500,000 jobs. The administration organized these special elections, which were held on different dates in each state. The national popular vote for repeal was 73 percent; in New York City the margin was more than 40 to 1. But even without urban votes, repeal would have won. Of the thirty-nine states that voted, all except the Carolinas rejected prohibition. Each state convention met on a different day, and all completed work in one day. On April 10, Michigan held the first state convention to ratify the amendment. Al Smith presided over the unanimously wet New York convention, which was broadcast on radio. Utah became the thirty-sixth and final state to complete ratification, on the afternoon of December 5, 1933, and the Twenty-First Amendment went into effect immediately. The amendment was ratified more quickly than any amendment in history. The WONPR held a celebratory dry dinner in Washington, DC, and immediately disbanded.

On March 4, 1933, shortly after Congress sent the Twenty-First Amendment to the states, Roosevelt was inaugurated. Just nine days later, while awaiting the amendment's ratification, Roosevelt proposed modification of the Volstead Act to allow beer that contained 3.2 percent alcohol. When the measure was introduced in the House, the gallery chanted, "Vote—vote—we want beer." A representative of the brewers argued, "In every glass there is a step forward toward prosperity." Roosevelt signed the Beer and Wine Revenue Act on March 22. He was determined that federal, state, and local governments could collect license fees and alcohol taxes as soon as possible, and the Federal Alcohol Control Administration was set up to enforce the law. This measure went into effect on April 7, 1933, the date that marked the end of prohibition in the minds of many people.

Anheuser-Busch delivered the first new case of beer to former governor Al Smith in New York City and sent several cases to President Roosevelt at the White House. Roosevelt's staff distributed the beer to the press corps. NBC and CBS radio covered the return of beer, and five major-league baseball teams announced that they would sell beer at their games. Within a year, 756 breweries had opened across America, although the number never reached prewar levels. Some of them had illegally produced beer during prohibition, but much of the beer came from familiar companies that had pursued other businesses during prohibition. Busch switched from soft drinks to beer quickly and already had a distribution system in place. Schlitz, which had made half a percent near-beer, started production immediately, but Pabst had sold its property and equipment and had to buy them back. Some giant breweries, such as Moerlein in Cincinnati, did not return.

Not every state was ready for the repeal of either the Volstead Act or the Eighteenth Amendment. State constitutions and laws had to be modified to conform to the new federal policy. In March 1933, only fourteen states were ready for legal beer. Many state

10. On April 7, 1933, the night that legal beer returned, the Fauerbach Drewery Tavern in Madison, Wisconsin, did a roaring business.

legislatures took up the alcohol issue in early 1933, but others decided to wait until the Twenty-First Amendment was ratified, as few people predicted that the amendment would be adopted so quickly. In May, Florida rushed to legalize and tax beer and light wine. The state had a long coastline open to rum-runners and was desperate for revenue with the decline of tourism. Previously dry newspapers clamored for the bill because they needed alcohol ads to survive the Depression. Distribution of distilled spirits was more contentious. In December, twenty-four states were ready to handle legal liquor. Policies ranged from the casual licensing of wide-open saloons in Nevada to the sale of hard liquor only for home consumption in state stores in Montana.

By early 1934, most states had acted to adopt new alcohol policies because every state needed tax revenue that wine and hard liquor could now provide. Meanwhile, the Roosevelt administration, as an economy move, had stopped enforcing prohibition by abolishing the hated Prohibition Bureau in the summer of 1933. In states with weak or nonexistent enforcement, prohibition ceased to exist in early 1933. Moonshiners and bootleggers thrived until the states and federal government passed licensing and tax laws. Although Florida had legalized beer in May 1933, the state did not repeal state constitutional prohibition until a referendum in November 1934. The Seattle City Council, desperate for revenue, licensed speakeasies in 1933, even though no state law authorized such a policy. When Washington State finally enacted a new state alcohol policy and tax in January 1934, the state was forced to concede revenue sharing with cities to get the bill passed.

Some states did make efforts to keep bootleggers from selling alcohol. Previous lawbreakers were not necessarily likely to conduct businesses according to the new state laws. Accordingly, Utah gave many of its licenses to Mormons on the grounds that they were pillars of the community who would uphold closing hours and drinking age laws. On the other hand, the alcohol industry retained its stigma, and many business leaders had no interest in being involved in a disreputable industry long condemned by evangelical Protestants. Washington State licensed speakeasies to sell beer but warned owners that any violations would bring the loss of a license. By 1941, one-quarter of the licenses had been revoked, mostly for selling Canadian bootleg liquor, for illegal sales on Sunday, or for sales to minors under twenty-one. In Templeton, Iowa, former moonshiner Joe Irlbeck got a tavern license in 1936. He later ran a beer wholesale company. Illinois more or less automatically licensed speakeasies. Owners were seen as valuable members of the community who had suffered from oppression during prohibition.

As the Roosevelt administration pursued repeal, John D. Rockefeller Jr. pondered what should replace prohibition. He decided that the federal government and the states needed to impose strong controls on alcohol sales. "If carefully made plans of control are not made," he wrote in the *New York Times*, "the old evils against which prohibition was invoked can easily return." Prohibition had been a reaction to the irresponsible, unregulated alcohol industry before World War I. The tied-house saloon had been the source of many social problems, and corrupt political machines rooted in those saloons had threatened democracy. Rockefeller knew that a majority of Americans did not want the return of the saloon, so he hired experts to study alcohol management in other nations, including Canada and Scandinavia, where robust government control of alcohol had been implemented as a substitute for prohibition.

Rockefeller's agents, Raymond Fosdick and Albert Scott, published their findings in *Toward Liquor Control* (1933). They argued that the federal government and state governments needed strong regulation of the alcohol industry to end the controversy over alcohol once and for all. When the book was published, major newspapers ran excerpts and reviews. Rockefeller had this book widely distributed to reporters, state legislators, and other decision makers. Rockefeller also commissioned his attorneys to draft model control laws, which became the basis for many state statutes. WONPR reinforced Rockefeller's call for strict regulation and suggested government manufacture and sale of alcohol, an idea that President Roosevelt personally favored. While WONPR worked for strong state controls, AAPA opposed tight regulation in favor of a free market in alcohol.

Several principles governed the Rockefeller report, as the book was widely called. First, each state that allowed the legal sale of alcohol needed a strong alcohol control board to write administrative rules, to enforce those rules, and to collect taxes and license fees. The alcohol industry needed to be subordinated to the state because alcohol was inherently dangerous. A free market in alcohol had the potential to (again) produce bad consequences. Before prohibition, state governments had rarely taxed or regulated alcohol, which cities and counties had controlled. Afraid that licensees would cheat on taxes based on quantities sold, local jurisdictions had issued numerous flat-fee licenses that encouraged vendors to push sales, particularly by selling to drunks and minors or in violation of Sunday closing laws. The large number of licenses made it hard for retailers to make a living. Because saloons were politically powerful, local elected officials and police usually ignored violations.

The report called for the new state control boards to insulate public policy from both industry and political pressure. The governor would appoint state board members for fixed terms, and confirmation by the state senate would be required. These appointed officials were protected from local corruption, and the governor could be held accountable for the board's behavior. Because the state would collect taxes at the wholesale level, tax cheating was minimized. Taxes would be levied on the amount of alcohol sold, which would raise prices, reduce sales, and discourage licensees from pursuing illegal sales. The board could revoke or suspend a holder's license for violating the law or board regulations without interference from local elected officials, and the number of licenses could be restricted to ensure that vendors could earn a decent living from legal sales.

Second, the report advised, both tax policy and rules about access should recognize that different beverages had different risks. Beer, which posed only a slight public danger, should be lightly taxed and widely available at licensed outlets for both on-premises and home consumption. Because it was bulky, cheap, and hard to hide, brewers were unlikely to cheat on taxes. Accordingly, private wholesalers were appropriate, and many retail licenses would be granted. Light wine consumed with food was also benign, but wine was strong enough that if it were imbibed by itself, trouble could result. Therefore, wine should be more highly taxed than beer, and it might be sold only in restaurants with meals or in state-owned or privately licensed stores for home consumption. Hard liquor was dangerous. It should be heavily taxed, and it should be sold only in a limited number of venues, perhaps only in a small number of state-owned stores for home consumption. The report, however, noted that different states had different needs, and no one policy could fit every state.

Third, the report urged every state to impose a three-tier system to separate the producer, wholesaler, and retailer. No financial connections were to be allowed across tiers. Loans or gifts were banned, and all transactions had to be paid immediately in cash. The purpose of this separation was to prevent the return of tied houses, which the report considered inevitable without these strict legal requirements. There were also practical reasons for the three-tier system. States could not effectively regulate or tax out-of-state producers. Distilling was concentrated in a few states, and economies of scale made widespread local distilling unlikely. Most wine was imported from outside the United States or came from California. Only beer was local, but national breweries were likely to gain a large market share in most states. To collect taxes effectively, states needed to deal with in-state wholesalers rather than producers. Wholesale taxes also made the wholesaler a private enforcer to monitor the retailer. Because there were thousands of outlets, collecting taxes at the retail level was far more difficult. Wholesale licenses would be much more lucrative than retail licenses, and wholesalers would be reluctant to dodge taxes or violate regulations that would lead to revocation of valuable licenses.

State control boards had to turn over alcohol taxes and license fees to the state government, which might redistribute part of the money to cities, but boards had less reason to worry about the loss of revenue from suspending or revoking licenses than any city government did. The report also urged states to consider state wholesaling and state-owned retail stores for hard liquor and wine. These beverages were seen as especially lucrative and exploitative of the public. "Only as the profit motive is eliminated," wrote Rockefeller in the introduction, "is there any hope of controlling the liquor traffic in the interest of a decent society." The public, however, was less keen on state control than was Rockefeller. While the public accepted control boards and three-tier distribution to stop tied houses, the majority of states adopted private wholesaling and retailing. To many dry Americans, the idea of a government-owned liquor store constituted state complicity with the devil. Wets were afraid that state stores would be poorly stocked with overpriced mediocre products, which did sometimes happen.

In November 1933, just before repeal became effective, the Roosevelt administration decided to regulate the alcohol industry by establishing the Federal Alcohol Control Administration. Until Congress could pass a new statute in 1934, beer, wine, and spirits were to be governed under the National Recovery Act (NRA). Separate NRA administrative codes covered beer, wine, and spirits. In other industries, leading producers drafted the code for each particular industry, but the administration wrote the three alcohol producer codes. Brewers, vintners, and distillers had to abide by certain manufacturing standards, and they had to recognize labor unions, but the most important provision in the new codes banned tied houses. The federal government licensed producers, distributers, and retailers separately, and the alcohol codes allowed no financial ties across these three tiers.

To mesh with federal policy, almost all states established state alcohol control boards to regulate the time, place, and manner of sales, and almost every state adopted the three-tier system to prevent tied-house saloons. Many states restricted retail licenses to stop cutthroat competition, regulated advertising, and fixed retail prices. While all states used private wholesale and retail licensees for beer, regulations about wine and hard liquor varied. States along the Canadian border worried about untaxed bootleg liquor from Canada, and moonshine was a chronic problem in Appalachia. Some states treated wine like beer, other states lumped wine with spirits, and still others put wine into a separate category, as the Rockefeller report had recommended. After the US Supreme Court voided the NRA, Congress incorporated most of the NRA code provisions for the alcohol industry into the Federal Alcohol Administration Act (1935), which established the Federal Alcohol Administration. In 1936 the $2.60 a gallon federal tax on distilled spirits and $5.00 a barrel tax on beer brought in 13 percent of federal tax revenues.

Although only a few states adopted exclusive state stores for wine, eighteen states adopted state store systems to sell hard liquor. In the popular vote on repeal, these were the states that had cast the highest percentage of dry votes. Fear of the return of statewide prohibition played a role in the adoption of state stores. Along the Canadian border, Maine, New Hampshire, Vermont, Michigan, Montana, and Washington wanted to stop untaxed, illegal Canadian imports. Washington influenced Oregon. Dry Mormons led Utah and Idaho to adopt state stores. Political patronage jobs in state stores were important in Pennsylvania and Ohio. Bible belt prohibitionists affected Iowa as well as West Virginia, Virginia, North Carolina, Alabama, and Mississippi. Wyoming used state control of wholesale hard liquor to raise maximum revenue, but retail sales were private. Maryland authorized several counties to operate county-run liquor stores.

Some state regulations bordered on the bizarre. Many were designed to forestall a new attempt to impose prohibition, which had been a political issue for a hundred years. To get a drink in Texas, the customer sometimes had to join a "private club," which was a euphemism for what looked like a saloon. California, predictably, had low taxes on wine, while Illinois, home of major distilleries, lightly taxed hard liquor. Wisconsin not only had low taxes on beer, but the age to purchase beer there was eighteen. Brewers hoped that by the time beer drinkers turned twenty-one, they would have little interest in spirits. Most states set the drinking age at twenty-one, but New York's minimum was eighteen, which made New York City a magnet for teenagers from

New Jersey and Connecticut. In the 1930s, hundreds of counties, particularly in the Bible Belt, had local option prohibition. Although most states quickly legalized alcohol to gain tax revenue, Oklahoma, Kansas, and Mississippi remained legally dry, except for beer, until after World War II. In 1966, Mississippi became the last state to drop prohibition.

Before prohibition, alcohol had been largely unregulated and lightly taxed. The result had been the emergence of powerful producers, sleazy tied houses, corrupt politics, alcohol abuse, crime, and family violence. Reformers had promised that prohibition would end drinking, corruption, crime, and poverty. Instead, the dry policy yielded bad, overpriced liquor; promoted lawlessness; enriched gangsters; and hurt government revenues. Prohibition certainly did not end drinking. By 1933, a disillusioned public was ready to try a different type of alcohol policy, one that stressed government control rather than a free market or prohibition. Under repeal, the United States established an effective state and federal regulatory system that acknowledged alcohol as an inherently dangerous product that needed to be monitored closely. Alcohol became widely available, but substantial taxes kept the price high enough to reduce consumption, state governments determined where alcohol was sold or consumed, and control boards decided the circumstances under which it was drunk.

Chapter 5
Legacies

The most important legacy of prohibition in the United States concerned a dramatic change in drinking habits. The raunchy all-male saloon did disappear for good, and per capita consumption of alcohol was reduced for a very long time. Consumption in the 1930s was one-third lower than before prohibition because people had little money to spend on drinks during the Great Depression and because a generation that had come of age during prohibition never imbibed much alcohol. An American born in 1900 could not drink legally until age thirty-three, past the age when use normally peaks. Consumption drops with each decade of adult life, and by age sixty-five a majority of people are abstainers.

Another legacy of repeal was the painful recognition within the alcohol industry that it could be toppled by public opinion; for years producers worried about the return of prohibition. To head off the possibility, they avoided promotions or portrayed alcohol as an innocent relaxant. When repeal took place in 1933, vintners and distillers agreed through their trade associations that they would not advertise on radio. But brewers did use radio and benefited from this distinction, which annoyed the vintners and distillers. Beer ads moved seamlessly from radio to television in the 1940s, and as beer sales continued to increase, vintners finally broke the taboo by advertising on television in the 1960s.

Distillers made a brief attempt to follow but received so much criticism that they backed off. Later, cable television allowed distillers to find a new way to access television. Indeed, television could be powerful. In the 1950s, Anheuser-Busch sponsored many sports programs to reach young male viewers and thus became the country's dominant brewer. In 1976, Schlitz was number two. Eager to gain market share, the company ran a short ad campaign in 1977 that was described sarcastically within the ad industry as Drink Schlitz or I'll Kill You. Sales dropped so rapidly that the brand vanished.

Even in the 1930s, the alcohol industry conceded that millions of people suffered from catastrophic drinking problems and that producers had a responsibility to try to reduce this harm. Accordingly, the industry sponsored scientific research on alcohol and alcoholism. The Yale Center of Alcohol Studies, founded in 1935, played a prominent role in this effort. Early research supported the disease model of addiction, and much of what we know today about drug reactions inside the brain began with rat studies at Yale. (In 1962 the center moved to Rutgers University.) After World War II, more robust funding came from the National Institutes of Health, which in 1974 created the National Institute on Alcohol Abuse and Alcoholism (NIAAA). Researchers developed effective drug treatments for alcohol dependency, for example, chlordiazepoxide (Librium) and Naltrexone.

Another legacy of prohibition came in 1935, when Bill Wilson and Dr. Bob Smith founded Alcoholics Anonymous (AA). AA rejected the prohibition model to place responsibility for drinking on the individual drinker. In many ways this movement resembled the Washingtonian self-help movement of the 1840s. During the early nineteenth century, the temperance movement had seen alcohol in moral terms, whereas prohibition turned alcohol into a social, cultural, and political issue. After the repeal of prohibition, alcohol abuse was increasingly identified as a therapeutic issue involving the individual. In AA's twelve-step method, the alcoholic had to admit the desire to drink, to accept personal responsibility, and to acknowledge the need for abstinence. AA eventually claimed millions of members around the world. In recent decades, the same method has been applied to other addictions.

Alcohol consumption rose during World War II both at home and abroad. Separation from loved ones, stressful defense work, and difficult military life all played roles in increased alcohol intake among both men and women. After the war this cohort continued to be hard drinkers. They favored beer, which was cheap, easy to obtain, and advertised frequently on television, but they also liked mixed drinks made with hard liquor. Their children, the older baby boomers, likewise drank beer and distilled spirits. In the late 1960s and early 1970s, the older boomers and their parents constituted two exceptionally heavy drinking generations that overlapped. Unlike their parents, boomers were also attracted to wine, which was cheaper than hard liquor. Many boomers thought that red wine went well with marijuana.

American alcohol consumption per capita rose from 1933 to 1973, when it passed the pre-prohibition level, and then peaked in 1980. Consumption began to decline when younger boomers in the 1980s turned away from both alcohol and drugs to embrace a healthy lifestyle that included natural foods, meditation, yoga, running, and working out in gyms. Along with the health movement, women entering the professional workforce in large numbers in the 1980s helped change both perceptions and practices about alcohol. Traditional hard-drinking professions such as journalism and advertising, known for the three-martini lunch, became more sober as women joined the ranks in large numbers. In most cultures, women drink much less than men.

Women may also have been influenced by the discovery of fetal alcohol syndrome, which NIAAA explored at a workshop in 1977. While researchers had long recognized that alcoholic mothers frequently gave birth to low-weight babies with developmental problems, the new research stressed that as little as one drink during a certain phase of early pregnancy could produce a negative outcome. Many women decided not to drink if they were pregnant or were trying to become pregnant. In 1988, the federal government began to require alcoholic beverage labels to contain health warnings, including warnings about pregnancy.

The 1980s also brought the rise of neo-prohibition, an organized movement to reduce per capita consumption of alcohol in the United States. For decades, experts had agreed that the percentage of people in a society who had the potential for serious alcohol problems was around 10 percent, with the exact percentage depending upon the definition of what constituted a serious drinking problem. In the 1970s, however, new research showed that a heavy drinking culture led to a higher percentage of the population being at risk for severe drinking problems. This finding led to a movement in the 1980s to reduce harms by lowering average consumption. Thus, an overall reduction in consumption would reduce the number of people injured by alcohol disorders.

Mothers Against Drunk Driving (MADD) headed this new anti-liquor movement, which had support inside the federal government. Candy Lightner founded MADD in 1980 after a drunk driver had killed her thirteen-year-old daughter. The driver, who had been arrested numerous times for drunk driving, received a suspended sentence. In addition to campaigning effectively for more serious penalties for drunk driving, MADD promoted the idea of a designated non-drinking driver within any group that was drinking. It also advocated that bars and restaurants be held liable for serving drunk customers, for a reduction in the level of blood alcohol considered to be proof of drunkenness, and for zero tolerance for blood alcohol for underage drinkers who were drivers. During the 1970s, a majority of states had dropped the drinking age to eighteen, sometimes with disastrous highway fatalities. MADD's most important accomplishment was to get federal legislation passed in 1984 to withhold highway funds from any state that did not raise its legal drinking age to twenty-one. By 1988, every state had done so. The point was to stop cross-border teenage drunk driving fatalities. Since 1988, annual drunk driving deaths have been cut in half; this reduction has saved 250,000 lives over twenty-five years.

Massive immigration during the 1980s and 1990s also played a role in declining per capita alcohol consumption in the United States. For the first time in American history, immigrants came not from Europe but from Mexico, from other places in the western hemisphere, and from Asia, all of which were light-drinking cultures. The states that had the greatest number of immigrants, California and New York, had the largest declines in per capita consumption, 36 and 37 percent, respectively.

Culture plays a major role in drinking attitudes and practices. Mexican American men drink about as much as their Anglo counterparts in their twenties, but they drink much less after marriage because more than half of Mexican American women are teetotalers. When one partner in a couple does not drink, the other partner drinks less. Young Mexican American men, like their Anglo counterparts, primarily imbibe beer. Many Asians have the alcohol flush gene, which causes small amounts of alcohol to produce an unpleasant hot flash. Persons with this gene or from areas where the gene is common tend to be abstainers. African Americans continue to be light drinkers, and half of black women do not drink. Muslim immigrants are unlikely to drink for religious reasons. Members of certain Native American tribes drink heavily, but the country's heartiest drinkers are white Americans who remain true to their European origins.

Per capita alcohol consumption in the United States started to rise after 1997, but consumer preferences also changed. The long-term slide in beer that began in 1981 continued to 2014, when consumption was 20 percent below the peak. On the other hand, wine consumption rose after 1993 and reached an all-time high in 2014. Wine particularly gained ground in parts of the country where little wine previously had been drunk. Millennials also discovered hard liquor, which increased in sales. Sweet mixed drinks appealed to a generation raised on soft drinks and sugary snacks. The three million veterans of the Afghanistan and Iraq wars proved to be hard drinkers.

Prohibition marked a curious episode in the history of drinking in America, as it did in other nations that tried to ban alcohol. Where the substance has not been part of local culture, prohibition has sometimes been effective, as has been true in some Islamic areas. On the other hand, people in hard-drinking cultures have usually resisted any ban so strongly that it has had to be repealed. After

Table 1. Per capita annual alcohol consumption by beverage type

Date	Beer	Wine	Spirits	All beverages
1850	0.14	0.08	1.88	2.10
1871–80	0.56	0.14	1.02	1.72
1906–10	1.47	0.17	0.96	2.60 (peak)
1935	0.68	0.09	0.43	1.20
1940	0.73	0.16	0.67	1.56
1950	1.04	0.23	0.77	2.04
1960	0.99	0.22	0.86	2.07
1970	1.14	0.27	1.11	2.52
1980	1.38	0.34	1.04	2.76 (peak)
1990	1.34	0.33	0.77	2.45
2000	1.22	0.31	0.64	2.17
2014	1.10	0.43	0.80	2.32

Source: US Department of Health and Human Services, National Institute of Alcohol Abuse and Alcoholism. "Surveillance Report #104: Apparent Per Capita Alcohol Consumption: National, State, and Regional Trends, 1977–2014" (2016), 12–13.

World War I, Vladimir Lenin restored the Russian state spirits monopoly. Liquor revenues have continued to finance the Russian government, even at the expense of low male life expectancy due to widespread alcoholism. After a short dry experiment at the end of World War I, Finland, Norway, and Canada abandoned prohibition amid empty government coffers and widespread illegal distillation. Always eager for revenue, governments have also tended to stop other restrictive anti-liquor policies over time. Sweden gave up the Gothenburg system's strict allotments of alcohol to individual drinkers, although it continues to use government outlets to sell hard liquor. Since the 1990s, Britain has lengthened hours of service in public houses, and youth binge drinking has soared. There are always trade-offs between harms to individuals or to society versus benefits in the form of government revenues and the popularity of easy access to alcohol. In those parts of the world where alcohol has long been part of local culture, prospects for significant restrictions remain doubtful.

References

Introduction

On Britain and Russia, respectively, see James Nicholls, *The Politics of Alcohol* (Manchester, UK: Manchester University Press, 2009) and Mark L. Schrad, *Vodka Politics* (New York: Oxford University Press, 2014).

Chapter 1

George Washington's 1755 election is in W. J. Rorabaugh, *The Alcoholic Republic* (New York: Oxford University Press, 1979), 152.

Hall quoted in Harrison Hall, *The Distiller*, 2nd ed. (Philadelphia: author, 1818), 17.

"The devil had an efficient hand..." appears in Huntington Lyman, *An Address Delivered before the Temperance Society of Franklinville* (New York: Sleight and Robinson, 1830), 5.

"We may set it down..." appears in Ashel Nettleton, "Spirit of the Pilgrims," in American Temperance Society, *Second Annual Report* (1829), 53.

"Daily experience convinces us..." quoted in Ian R. Tyrrell, *Sobering Up* (Westport, CT: Greenwood Press, 1979), 137.

Wise quoted in Henry A. Wise, *The Life of Henry A. Wise of Virginia, 1806–1876* (New York: Macmillan, 1899), 74.

New York State votes for 1846 are in Thomas R. Pegram, *Battling Demon Rum* (Chicago: Ivan R. Dee, 1998), 38.

Chapter 2

The Women's Crusade is in Jack S. Blocker, *Give to the Winds Thy Fears* (Westport, CT: Greenwood Press, 1985).

On Willard, see Ruth Bordin, *Frances Willard* (Chapel Hill: University of North Carolina Press, 1986).

On the World's WCTU, see Ian R. Tyrrell, *Woman's World/Woman's Empire* (Chapel Hill: University of North Carolina Press, 1991).

Prohibition Party statistics are in Lisa M. F. Andersen, *The Politics of Prohibition* (New York: Cambridge University Press, 2013), 283.

Tennessee Methodists and Georgia Baptists quoted in Joe L. Coker, *Liquor in the Land of the Lost Cause* (Lexington: University Press of Kentucky, 2007), 61, 62.

"When there is a vigorous public sentiment…" quoted in Ann-Marie E. Szymanski, *Pathways to Prohibition* (Durham, NC: Duke University Press, 2003), 2.

"No workingman ever drank…" quoted in Lisa McGirr, *The War on Alcohol* (New York: Norton, 2016), 8.

"Alien illiterates rule our cities…" quoted in ibid., 17.

"The entire fabric of the Territory…" quoted in Elliott West, *The Saloon on the Rocky Mountain Mining Frontier* (Lincoln: University of Nebraska Press, 1979), 2.

On Native Americans and federal alcohol policy, see William E. Unrau, *White Man's Wicked Water* (Lawrence: University Press of Kansas, 1996), 103–116.

Leslie Keeley quoted in *I've Been to Dwight* (Dwight, IL: Dwight Historical Society, 2016), 2.

"We must create the appetite…" quoted in James H. Timberlake, *Prohibition and the Progressive Movement, 1900–1920* (New York: Atheneum, 1970), 111.

Mark Matthews quoted in Norman H. Clark, *Deliver Us from Evil* (New York: Norton, 1976), 4.

"It is the degenerate vote…" quoted in McGirr, *War on Alcohol*, 17.

"If we wish to purify politics…" quoted in Michael A. Lerner, *Dry Manhattan* (Cambridge, MA: Harvard University Press, 2007), 24.

On Nation, see Fran Grace, *Carry A. Nation* (Bloomington: Indiana University Press, 2001).

On the Anti-Saloon League, see K. Austin Kerr, *Organized for Prohibition* (New Haven: Yale University Press, 1985).

"It is the plain church-going people…" appears in Robert Woods, "Winning the Other Half," *Survey*, December 30, 1916, 352.

"Reforms are not revolutionary," quoted in Szymanski, *Pathways to Prohibition*, 3.

"Put the ballot in the hands of woman..." appears in "Warm Words to Help Suffrage," *Los Angeles Times*, September 18, 1911, section 2, 2.

Billy Sunday appears in "Sunday Talks Prohibition," *New York Times*, May 3, 1915, 18.

Clarence Darrow quoted in Clark, *Deliver Us from Evil*, 100.

"A national evil requires a national remedy," appears in "For National Prohibition," *New York Times*, November 9, 1917, 9.

"Alcohol is a narcotic..." quoted in McGirr, *War on Alcohol*, 19.

"Kansas has prohibition..." appears in "Renewal of the Contest for Prohibition," *Los Angeles Times*, January 28, 1915, section 2, 4.

Boston Transcript quoted in "The Supreme Court on Prohibition," *Los Angeles Times*, January 25, 1917, section 2, 4.

"The great American hotel..." appears in "Prohibition's Ghost Laid by Hotel Men," *New York Times*, November 24, 1916, 11.

Chicago's wet parade and Hobson's ridicule quoted in McGirr, *War on Alcohol*, 43, 44.

"The success of the mail order business..." appears in "Drinking on the Increase," *New York Times*, May 15, 1910, 2.

On alcohol taxes, see Bruce G. Carruthers, "The Semantics of Sin Tax: Politics, Morality, and Fiscal Imposition," *Fordham Law Review* 84 (2016): 2580–2581; L. Ames Brown, "Economics of Prohibition," *North American Review* 203, no. 723 (1916): 264.

"The principles of war are the same..." quoted in McGirr, *War on Alcohol*, 4.

"We deem it particularly deplorable..." appears in "Sees Prohibition Waning," *New York Times*, February 4, 1916, 13.

"Wholesale fraud" appears in "Both Sides Claiming Victory," *Los Angeles Times*, July 24, 1911, section 1, 2.

On the Texas election, see Lewis L. Gould, *Progressives and Prohibitionists* (Austin: University of Texas Press, 1973).

"The liquor traffic...is the strong financial supporter of the German-American Alliance," appears in "For National Prohibition," 9.

"The question for every American citizen..." quoted in Sabine Meyer, *We Are What We Drink* (Urbana: University of Illinois Press, 2015), 190.

"Shall the many have food..." appears in "War Prohibition Now!" *Independent*, May 26, 1917, 360.

"Conditions [are] worse here..." quoted in Meyer, *We Are What We Drink*, 184.

Elizabeth Tilton quoted in McGirr, *War on Alcohol*, 35.

William Randolph Hearst quoted in Kathleen Drowne, *Spirits of Defiance* (Columbus: Ohio State University Press, 2005), 18.

"The un-American, pro-German…treasonable liquor traffic," quoted in Lerner, *Dry Manhattan*, 31.

Chapter 3

On Carroll County, see Bryce T. Bauer, *Gentlemen Bootleggers* (Chicago: Chicago Review Press, 2014).

"Absolutely crooked," quoted in Michael A. Lerner, *Dry Manhattan* (Cambridge, MA: Harvard University Press, 2007), 71.

"The federal men…" appears in "Cabaret," *Variety*, July 14, 1922, 11.

The Ku Klux Klan minister and the *Fiery Cross* quoted in Lisa McGirr, *The War on Alcohol* (New York: Norton, 2016), 134, 136.

On moonshiners and stock car racing, see Daniel S. Pierce, *Real NASCAR* (Chapel Hill: University of North Carolina Press, 2010).

"The working classes demand their beer," appears in "Beer Approved, Whisky Doomed," *Los Angeles Times*, April 30, 1920, section 1, 4.

"If you really want to know…" quoted in Daniel Okrent, *Last Call* (New York: Scribner, 2010), 251.

Edward Edwards quoted in ibid., 287.

"Texas will not be bone dry…" appears in "Decrease in Crime," *Los Angeles Times*, January 9, 1922, section 1, 1.

"What is a mile or two extra?" appears in "Seizure Annoys Rum Row," *Los Angeles Times*, November 29, 1923, section 1, 4.

On Atlantic City smuggling, see the television series *Boardwalk Empire*.

"Only Capone kills like that," quoted in Edward D. Sullivan, *Rattling the Cup on Chicago Crime* (New York: Vanguard Press, 1929), 193.

"Some of them [bootleggers] deserve a good killing…" quoted in Philip Metcalfe, *Whispering Wires* (Portland, OR: Inkwater Press, 2007), 262.

"When the governor of the largest state…" quoted in David Farber, *Everybody Ought to Be Rich* (New York: Oxford University Press, 2013), 227.

"Governor Smith and that bunch of Tammany roughnecks…" appears in "Billy Sunday Flays Wets," *Los Angeles Times*, September 3, 1923, section 2, 1.

On the U.S. Supreme Court, see Robert Post, "Federalism, Passive Law, and the Emergence of the American Administrative State:

Prohibition and the Taft Court Era," *William and Mary Law Review* 48, no.1 (2006): 1–183.

"When licenses to sell liquor…" appears in "City's Prohibition Farce," *New York Times*, February 5, 1922, 89.

"The first day we opened…" quoted in Lerner, *Dry Manhattan*, 82–83.

"Soon after 1920, raving hordes of women…" quoted in McGirr, *War on Alcohol*, 108.

"As free with their persons…" appears in "Is Times Square Wild?" *Variety*, December 29, 1926, 25.

"She is the first woman in history…" appears in Helen B. Lowry, "New York's After-Midnight Clubs," *New York Times Book Review and Magazine*, February 5, 1922, 25.

"Never before has there ever been…" quoted in Lerner, *Dry Manhattan*, 143.

On Harlem speakeasies, see ibid., 131–132, 199–226; McGirr, *War on Alcohol*, 110–115.

"The Grape Growers are not held responsible…" quoted in Okrent, *Last Call*, 335.

"The fashionable rich demand their rum…" quoted in Kathleen Drowne, *Spirits of Defiance* (Columbus: Ohio State University Press, 2005), 133.

New York World quoted in "Prohibition That Prohibits," *Los Angeles Times*, May 28, 1925, A4.

"If they do not like the way…" quoted in Lerner, *Dry Manhattan*, 117.

"They say we should cultivate respect…" quoted in Drowne, *Spirits of Defiance*, 10.

"I have been fighting the liquor traffic…" quoted in Robert A. Hohner, *Prohibition and Politics* (Columbia: University of South Carolina Press, 1999), 223.

On Mexican American bootleggers, see McGirr, *War on Alcohol*, 92–93.

On alcohol consumption during prohibition, see Jeffrey A. Miron and Jeffrey Zwiebel, "Alcohol Consumption during Prohibition," *American Economic Review* 81, no. 2 (1991): 242–247. See also Angela K. Dills and Jeffrey A. Miron, "Alcohol Prohibition and Cirrhosis," *American Law and Economics Review* 6, no. 2 (2004): 285–318; Angela K. Dills, Mireille A. Jacobson, and Jeffrey A. Miron, "The Effect of Alcohol Prohibition on Alcohol Consumption: Evidence from Drunkenness Arrests," *Economics Letters* 86, no. 2 (2005): 279–284.

Chapter 4

Morris Sheppard quoted in Daniel Okrent, *Last Call* (New York: Scribner, 2010), 330.

"There was a large group..." quoted in Kenneth D. Rose, *American Women and the Repeal of Prohibition* (New York: New York University Press, 1996), 77.

"Telling citizens what they must..." quoted in Caryn E. Neumann, "The End of Gender Solidarity," *Journal of Women's History*, 9, no. 2 (1997): 38.

"I represent the women of America..." quoted in Rose, *American Women and the Repeal of Prohibition*, 9.

"Little group of wine-drinking society women" quoted in ibid., 83.

"When women entered the fight..." appears in "Smith Sees Repeal Possible This Fall," *New York Times*, August 2, 1933, 18.

"I know of nothing since...woman's suffrage..." quoted in Michael A. Lerner, *Dry Manhattan* (Cambridge, MA: Harvard University Press, 2007), 197.

"This convention wants repeal," quoted in Norman H. Clark, *Deliver Us from Evil* (New York: Norton, 1976), 205.

"The taxpayer has paid the police..." appears in "House Has Frenzied Day," *New York Times*, February 21, 1933, 1.

Clarence Darrow quoted in Okrent, *Last Call*, 234.

"Vote-Vote-We want beer" quoted in Lerner, *Dry Manhattan*, 303.

"In every glass..." appears in "Cullen Predicts 300,000 Beer Jobs," *New York Times*, March 20, 1933, 3.

"If carefully made plans of control..." appears in "Rockefeller Lists Aims after Repeal," *New York Times*, October 6, 1933, 4.

"Only as the profit motive is eliminated..." appears in Harry G. Levine, "The Birth of American Alcohol Control," *Contemporary Drug Problems* 12, no. 1 (1985): 90.

Further reading

Andersen, Lisa M. F. *The Politics of Prohibition: American Governance and the Prohibition Party, 1869–1933*. New York: Cambridge University Press, 2013.

Bauer, Bryce T. *Gentlemen Bootleggers: The True Story of Templeton Rye, Prohibition, and a Small Town in Cahoots*. Chicago: Chicago Review Press, 2014.

Bergreen, Laurence. *Capone: The Man and the Era*. New York: Simon & Schuster, 1994.

Berliner, Louise. *Texas Guinan: Queen of the Nightclubs*. Austin: University of Texas Press, 1993.

Berridge, Virginia. *Demons: Our Changing Attitudes to Alcohol, Tobacco, and Drugs*. Oxford, UK: Oxford University Press, 2013.

Blee, Kathleen M. *Women of the Klan: Racism and Gender in the 1920s*. Berkeley: University of California Press, 1991.

Blocker, Jack S., Jr., David M. Fahey, and Ian R. Tyrrell, eds. *Alcohol and Temperance in Modern History: An International Encyclopedia*. 2 vols. Santa Barbara, CA: ABC-CLIO, 2003.

Brown, Dorothy M. *Mabel Walker Willebrandt*. Knoxville: University of Tennessee Press, 1984.

Clark, Norman H. *Deliver Us from Evil: An Interpretation of American Prohibition*. New York: Norton, 1976.

Coker, Joe L. *Liquor in the Land of the Lost Cause: Southern White Evangelicals and the Prohibition Movement*. Lexington: University Press of Kentucky, 2007.

Courtwright, David T. *Forces of Habit: Drugs and the Making of the Modern World*. Cambridge, MA: Harvard University Press, 2001.

Drowne, Kathleen. *Spirits of Defiance: National Prohibition and Jazz Age Literature, 1920–1933*. Columbus: Ohio State University Press, 2005.

Goyens, Tom. *Beer and Revolution: The German Anarchist Movement in New York City, 1880–1914*. Urbana: University of Illinois Press, 2007.

Guthrie, John J., Jr. "Rekindling the Spirits: From National Prohibition to Local Option in Florida, 1928–1935." *Florida Historical Quarterly* 74, no. 1 (1995): 23–39.

Hamm, Richard F. *Shaping the Eighteenth Amendment: Temperance Reform, Legal Culture, and the Polity, 1880–1920*. Chapel Hill: University of North Carolina Press, 1995.

Kerr, K. Austin. *Organized for Prohibition: A New History of the Anti-Saloon League*. New Haven, CT: Yale University Press, 1985.

Kyvig, David E. *Repealing National Prohibition*. 2nd ed. Kent, OH: Kent State University Press, 2000.

Lerner, Michael A. *Dry Manhattan: Prohibition in New York City*. Cambridge, MA: Harvard University Press, 2007.

Levine, Harry G. "The Birth of American Alcohol Control: Prohibition, the Power Elite, and the Problem of Lawlessness." *Contemporary Drug Problems* 12, no. 1 (1985): 63–115.

Levine, Harry G., and Craig Reinarman. "From Prohibition to Regulation: Lessons from Alcohol Policy for Drug Policy." *Milbank Quarterly* 69, no. 3 (1991): 461–494.

Lewis, Michael. *The Coming of Southern Prohibition: The Dispensary System and the Battle over Liquor in South Carolina, 1907–1915*. Baton Rouge: Louisiana State University Press, 2016.

Mappen, Marc. *Prohibition Gangsters: The Rise and Fall of a Bad Generation*. New Brunswick, NJ: Rutgers University Press, 2013.

McGirr, Lisa. *The War on Alcohol: Prohibition and the Rise of the American State*. New York: Norton, 2016.

Metcalfe, Philip. *Whispering Wires: The Tragic Tale of an American Bootlegger*. Portland, OR: Inkwater Press, 2007.

Meyer, Sabine N. *We Are What We Drink: The Temperance Battle in Minnesota*. Urbana: University of Illinois Press, 2015.

Miller, Wilbur R. *Revenuers and Moonshiners: Enforcing Federal Liquor Law in the Mountain South, 1865–1900*. Chapel Hill: University of North Carolina Press, 1991.

Miron, Jeffrey A., and Jeffrey Zwiebel. "Alcohol Consumption during Prohibition." *American Economic Review* 81, no. 2 (1991): 242–247.

Moore, Leonard J. *Citizen Klansmen: The Ku Klux Klan in Indiana, 1921–1928*. Chapel Hill: University of North Carolina Press, 1991.

National Institute on Alcohol Abuse and Alcoholism (NIAAA) website. www.niaaa.nih.gov.

Okrent, Daniel. *Last Call: The Rise and Fall of Prohibition*. New York: Scribner, 2010.

Osborn, Matthew W. *Rum Maniacs: Alcoholic Insanity in the Early American Republic*. Chicago: University of Chicago Press, 2014.

Pegram, Thomas R. *Battling Demon Rum: The Struggle for a Dry America, 1800–1933*. Chicago: Ivan R. Dee, 1998.

Phillips, Roderick. *Alcohol: A History*. Chapel Hill: University of North Carolina Press, 2014.

Pierce, Daniel S. *Real NASCAR: White Lightning, Red Clay, and Big Bill France*. Chapel Hill: University of North Carolina Press, 2010.

Post, Robert. "Federalism, Passive Law, and the Emergence of the American Administrative State: Prohibition and the Taft Court Era." *William and Mary Law Review* 48, no. 1 (2006): 1–183.

Powers, Madelon. *Faces along the Bar: Lore and Order in the Workingman's Saloon, 1870–1920*. Chicago: University of Chicago Press, 1998.

Rockaway, Robert. "The Notorious Purple Gang: Detroit's All-Jewish Prohibition Era Mob." *Shofar: An Interdisciplinary Journal of Jewish Studies* 20, no. 1 (2001): 113–130.

Rorabaugh, W. J. *The Alcoholic Republic: An American Tradition*. New York: Oxford University Press, 1979.

Rorabaugh, W. J. "The Origins of the Washington State Liquor Control Board, 1934." *Pacific Northwest Quarterly* 100, no. 4 (2009): 159–168.

Rose, Kenneth D. *American Women and the Repeal of Prohibition*. New York: New York University Press, 1996.

Szymanski, Ann-Marie E. *Pathways to Prohibition: Radicals, Moderates, and Social Movement Outcomes*. Durham, NC: Duke University Press, 2003.

Thompson, Peter. *Rum Punch and Revolution: Taverngoing and Public Life in Eighteenth-Century Philadelphia*. Philadelphia: University of Pennsylvania Press, 1999.

Tyrrell, Ian R. *Sobering Up: From Temperance to Prohibition in Antebellum America, 1800–1860*. Westport, CT: Greenwood Press, 1979.

Tyrrell, Ian R. *Woman's World/Woman's Empire: The Woman's Christian Temperance Union in International Perspective, 1880-1930*. Chapel Hill: University of North Carolina Press, 1991.

Unrau, William E. *White Man's Wicked Water: The Alcohol Trade and Prohibition in Indian Country, 1802-1892*. Lawrence: University Press of Kansas, 1996.

US Department of Health and Human Services, National Institute on Alcohol Abuse and Alcoholism. *Alcohol Use among U.S. Ethnic Minorities*. Rockville, MD: NIAAA, 1989.

US Department of Health and Human Services, National Institute on Alcohol Abuse and Alcoholism. "Surveillance Report #104: Apparent Per Capita Alcohol Consumption: National, State, and Regional Trends, 1977-2014" (2016). http://pubs.niaaa.nih.gov/publications/surveillance.htm. Used November 2, 2016.

US Department of Health and Human Services, National Institute on Alcohol Abuse and Alcoholism. *Women and Alcohol Use*. Washington: US Department of Health and Human Services, 1988.

West, Elliott. *The Saloon on the Rocky Mountain Mining Frontier*. Lincoln: University of Nebraska Press, 1979.

Zimmerman, Jonathan. *Distilling Democracy: Alcohol Education in America's Public Schools, 1880-1925*. Lawrence: University Press of Kansas, 1999.

Index

ONLINE CATALOGUE
A Very Short Introduction

Our online catalogue is designed to make it easy to find your ideal Very Short Introduction. View the entire collection by subject area, watch author videos, read sample chapters, and download reading guides.

http://fds.oup.com/www.oup.co.uk/general/vsi/index.html

SOCIAL MEDIA
Very Short Introduction

Join our community
www.oup.com/vsi

- Join us online at the official Very Short Introductions
  Facebook page.
- Access the thoughts and musings of our authors with our
  online **blog**.
- Sign up for our monthly **e-newsletter** to receive information
  on all new titles publishing that month.
- Browse the full range of Very Short Introductions online.
- Read **extracts** from the Introductions for free.
- Visit our library of **Reading Guides**. These guides, written by our
  expert authors will help you to question again, why you think
  what you think.
- If you are a teacher or lecturer you can order inspection
  copies quickly and simply via our website.